MW01170944

JOURNEY TO SELFULLNESS

WRITTEN BY:

TASSILI MATA ATMA MA'AT

This book or parts thereof may not be reproduced in any form, stored in a retrieval system, or transmitted in any form by any means – electronic, mechanical, photocopy, recording, or otherwise – without prior written permission of the publisher, except as provided by United States of America copyright law.

The ideas, procedures, and suggestions in this book are not intended as a substitute for consulting with your physician. All matters regarding your health require medical supervision. Neither author nor the publisher shall be liable or responsible for any loss or damage allegedly arising from any information or suggestion in this book.

Visit the author's website at www.TassilisRawReality.com
All social media can be found: @TassilisRaw @IamAscension @TassiliMaat
Copyright @2021
ISBN: 979-8411118773
All rights reserved
Cover Design created by: Jimi Figz
Editors: StudioSteffanie Enterprises, Inc. and Olimatta Taal
Published by: **StudioSteffanie Enterprises, Inc.**

PREFACE

Welcome to your personal journey within!

It is a journey to self-fulfillment... Selfullness! Thank you for allowing me to be your guide. I am with you to assist you in remembering what you really already know. We'll begin with snippets of my journey to selfullness, so as to discover a common starting point. You will then ask yourself some questions as you affirm through daily affirmations, your remembrance. THERE ARE NO WRONG ANSWERS, as I invite you to journal daily for this full lunar cycle. Yes... 360° of inquiry in discovery of you.

None of it is mandatory; however, you are encouraged to create your own daily discipline by using these tools to assist you in your 'remembering' process. This workbook is even set up so you can continue for an entire solar cycle too. That's right! Another 360° as a continuum, as life is ontological. The goal is balance, a healthy homeostasis! Selfullness! In fact, you could come to know yourself so well that you just might be unrecognizable to even you. Couples doing this journey together have the opportunity to really get to know not only themselves, they can discover each other as true reflections of each other! If you have discovered on your journey to within that there are some deeper experiences than you can handle by yourself, please seek professional counseling. While 'The Journey to Selfullness' assists the healing process, I'm not a doctor. Remember, there is strength in numbers. Wherever two or more are gathered, there is the presence of the I Am! Thank you, again, for joining me on this journey within and this journey to self-fulfillment. This is your journey to selfullness. Your personal journey awaits you and your innermost thoughts!

In truth, In light, In love, Tassili Mata Atma Ma'at

PROLOGUE

Time... a succession of rhythms with a designated beginning and end. This being according to who or what is determining the said beginning or end. For example, the changing of the seasons, location on the globe, tilting of the earth's axis, the location of the sun, all contribute to the seasonal changes or rhythms. There is a clear beginning and end determined by the solstices and equinoxes. Although there is always a period of overlapping or blending where the weather will gradually get warmer or cooler. Leaves change colors and 'leave' (fall); i.e., the fall or autumn. Or they will bud and become new leaves or flower blossoms. There are, of course, some places on earth where change is based on raining or not. And trees stay green all year round. While somewhere else, there is only heat and getting hotter. Those seasons are in alignment with the poles shifting on the planet.

There are also man-made environmental influences that are speeding up the shifting or blending. All the while in a galactic sense there is no beginning or end, only time as a continuum. So, again we must consider who is determining what and when. Within the realm of our daily lives, we have sunrise and sunset. The clock is determined by the basic rhythm of the sun. However, in America there are several time realities operating simultaneously, EST, CST, and PST. There is also Daylight Saving Times as another example of this. As the story goes, William Willet, who created daylight savings time, decided to play with the agreed-upon time so the world would actually have more time for recreation. Ben Franklin got involved with this, pushing the idea. The US government tried it officially on March 31, 1918, as a wartime measure because, of course, the soldiers needed more time to fight. SMH! The farmers didn't like it and had it repealed in 1919. But the merchants did like it and it returned during World War II. After the war it was observed only in urban areas. In 1963, the United States was described as a chaos of clocks by the rest of the world. In 1966, the Uniform Time Act was passed to standardize time. Only the Indigenous people of America, Hawaii, Arizona, Puerto Rico, Guam, Samoa, and the US Virgin Islands observe natural sun time. And even among them, there are some who still honor Daylight Savings Time.

My point upheld, time is a perspective; a collective agreement and in actuality polyrhythmic. So, what rhythm moves you? What brings you into alignment, in harmony, on beat or off? On this journey, we will learn to dance to a few of the polyrhythms of the universe.

One verse, one song with layers of rhythms!

TABLE OF CONTENTS

Tassili Ma'at standing in front of a statute of Kwame Nkrumah, who liberated Ghana from colonial rule. His quote is one of my favorites:

"A country can rise no higher than the consciousness of its women!"

INTRODUCTION

This book is about life - a journey in it, through it, and as it. It's a series of steps, I took which lead me to my path of Wholistic Wellbeing. As a natural born melanated-indigenous woman, I am an Urban Mystic. I was born empathic and began my spiritual journey at an early age. I had two Wasbeens (ex-husbands), though not at the same time. LOL! I've given birth to six children, out of them, one did not stay. I raised five, mostly as a single mom to be healthy contributors to life. I have six amazing grandchildren so far. I am a Renaissance woman living as an Artist of Life. I earned a BFA degree from University of California San Diego. I am a community activist, yogini, a tantrica, a spiritual counselor and teacher. I am a Healer using food as medicine, deliciously! As a BOSS (Being Open to Successful Service), I have been a successful entrepreneur for 40 years just to share a bit of my Urban Mystic realm.

My philosophy of life is that "*Wholistic Well-being is a moving meditation of sustainable self-fulfillment. It's what I call being "Selfull."*" In this book you're invited to create that as your possibility, too. 'Selfullness' is neither selfish nor selfless. It is a balanced love of self. Being 'Selfull' isn't always easy though. In fact, I am always, in all ways, constantly consciously, in focus of mindfulness. Yes! It is true, it's work, it is a labor of love. I found some ways that help me to maintain 'Selfullness' as Wholistic Well-being and I'm going to share them with you in this workbook.

This 30-day journey begins with the new moon. Throughout each day of the lunar cycle there will be journaling, affirmations, and stories to affirm and inspire 'Selfullness' in you. Daily journaling, if done diligently, will help unlock the Goddess/God code DNA that is your Divine Birthright. In other words this book is a journey to within, to help you remember what you really already know. While this book is channeled through me as a natural born melanated woman, the healing activities can be done by women and men. In fact, there's even more powerful healing when done together.

As a reflection of each other, I see us as one. The Ancients called this "Ubuntu… I am because we are, we are therefore I am." In fact, if you are reading this, you are probably much further along on your path than I was at your age! Hmmm! How would I even know your age to say that?!?! LOL! Well, trust and know, as Spirits we're having a human experience. We are intuitive. We are always in a state of flux. We are either remembering - forgetting, applying - withholding, or reflecting - deflecting. Always balancinghappy and sad - complacent and motivated - lethargic and invigorated - disturbed and peaceful - angry and joyful, along with a myriad of other statesof being until we come to stasis; homeostasis, a healthy wholistic well-being, or 'Selfullness' to be exact. You will find tools and systems to establish and sustain this and more in these pages.

I'm so thankful to have this opportunity to be a vessel for the ancestors to pour into me and me into you. Thanks in advance for receiving this legacy. It is a sacred trust born of natural melanated indigenous woman ways. I write this so that our future generations can experience a continuum of wisdom, beauty, love and life. The way nature planned it. In the spirit of Truth, Order, Balance, Harmony, Justice, Reciprocity and Propriety. I invite you to join me, Tassili Ma'at, on the journey of Wholistic Well-Being into 'Selfullness!'

AFFIRMATIONS

This journal of Affirmations is designed to begin before the beginning of the new moon. And it ends after the end of the lunar cycle. This is so you will have an overlapping of time to transition to it and out of it. So, if you have purchased this journal in the middle of the lunar cycle, please be patient and wait for the natural cycle of universal flow so as to fully align yourself.

I am Spirit... Giving Birth to Myself... Affirmations

Day 0 I AM Spirit Giving Birth to Myself...I AM that I AM! Blackness... Consciousness... Before the Beginning... I AM!

Day 1 I AM Spirit Giving Birth to Myself...I AM that I AM in the Black Hole Moon Womb... I AM being!

Day 2 I AM Spirit Giving Birth to Myself... In the beginning I AM creating...I AM!

Day 3 I AM Spirit Giving Birth to Myself... I AM Creating "creating"... I go into the Endarkening...There IS light... I AM!

Day 4 I AM Spirit Giving Birth to Myself... I AM the Endarkening... I AM the light... I AM that I AM... I AM that I AM Being and I AM that I AM Not!

Day 5 I AM Spirit Giving Birth to Myself... Awareness... I Will willingly... I AM that I AM... The Self of my Self's creation... I AM!

Day 6 I AM Spirit Giving Birth to Myself... I AM light... I AM the Star... I AM the Seed of Being... I AM!

Day 7 I AM Spirit Giving Birth to Myself... I AM the Blackness... I AM the Dark Matter Soil of my Soul in which I plant the Starseed of myself... I AM!

Day 8 I AM Spirit Giving Birth to Myself... I AM the Movement that is the wave of the dark waters of Cosmic Womb Ocean... I AM the sacred waters of life saturating my Starseed Self... I AM!

Day 9 I AM Spirit Giving Birth to Myself... I Am Reverberations of eb and flow... I create the warmth of the heat I AM... I AM nurturing my Starseed Self in the soul of my soul... I AM!

Day 10 I AM Spirit Giving Birth to Myself... I AM that I AM Cultivating "cultivating" my Starseed Self... I AM!

Day 11 I AM Spirit Giving Birth to Myself... I AM that I AM formulation of my Starseed Self... I AM!

Day 12 I AM Spirit Giving Birth to Myself... I AM that I AM pushing through my soul's soil... Taking the form of that which is in formation... My Starseed Self fills with expansion... I AM!

Day 13 I AM Spirit Giving Birth to Myself... I AM that I AM that I AM Starseed of myself actualizing fullness... I AM!

Day 14 I AM Spirit Giving Birth to Myself... I AM that I AM the Starseed of my 'self' born again into my self's full materialization from the soil of my soul's light... I AM!

Day 15 I AM Spirit Giving Birth to Myself... I AM that I AM... I see myself as 'my' 'self'... Starseed (your name) I embrace ALL of me. I unapologetically shine... I AM that I AM!

Day 16 What are you giving birth to? I AM Spirit Giving Birth to Myself... I AM that I AM... Asè, Ahò, Amen, Amom, Ameen, In Lak'ech Ala K'in, Ubuntu, Namaste, Medasi ma nkwa, Nuk Pu Nu, Ani ze ani, Selah, Sat Nam... I AM THAT I AM!

Day 17 I AM Spirit Giving Birth to Myself... I AM that I AM... So, Who Am I? (Self-assessment) Because I AM that... I AM Starseed! I AM!

Day 18 I AM Spirit Giving Birth to Myself... I AM here on purpose... I came here to (Whatever shows up as your life's purpose. Even if you don't know yet, what do you think it is? What do you like to do and do well?) I AM Starseed. I shine on purpose. I AM that I AM the light. I AM!

Day 19 I AM Spirit Giving Birth to Myself... I AM that I AM the acknowledgment of my accomplishments in the cultivation in the soil of my soul... (List Them) I AM Starseed. I AM Accomplishment. I AM this that I AM!

Day 20 I AM Spirit Giving Birth to Myself... I AM that I AM accountable for my choices in my life. I AM the acknowledgment of what works as well as what does not work in my life. I shine with gratitude for lessons learned. I AM Starseed the common denominator of my destiny... I AM!

Day 21 I AM Spirit Giving Birth to Myself... I AM that I AM the balance... The balance is all the feather seeks... We are perfect in our imperfection... I AM that I AM Starseed... Whole.Complete. Perfect. I AM that I AM my perfect imperfections... I AM!

Day 22 I AM Spirit Giving Birth to Myself... The feather and the heart of the soul of Starseed sees only itself first. I AM that I AM my truth... I AM!

Day 23 I AM Spirit Giving Birth to Myself...The heart is heavy unless one takes themselves lightly... I AM releasing shame and embarrassment by learning from the sh*t of life. I AM the knowledge that is the fertilizer reconditioning the soil of my soul... Life is too short not to shine Starseed. Intentions of a pure heart are those nurtured in the richness of the Soil of the Soul's knowing of mistakes and misdeeds done. I AM that I AM learning to fertilize and grow out of the sh*t! I AM!

Day 24 I AM Spirit Giving Birth to Myself... I AM that I AM the integrity of my shine. The integrity of my shine is found in the accountability that my soul is nurtured in... Alone in my own sh*t, I AM acknowledging the "ALL ONENESS" of it all. I AM Starseed. I AM that I AM my own sh*t! I AM!

Day 25 I AM Spirit Giving Birth to Myself... I AM acknowledging. I alone as the "ALL ONE" Know what is workable and what is not... I AM that I AM my observations... I AM!

Day 26 I AM Spirit Giving Birth to Myself... I see... I AM Starseed as the light that I AM... I turn to my inner eye introspection... I enter the spectrum of my inner sanctum... I AM that I AM my first eye. I AM!

Day 27 I AM Spirit Giving Birth to Myself... I go into the Endarkening. I see beyond sight... I reflect my inner light into myself... I AM the sacred sanctum of the Soil of my Soul... I AM reflecting the inner realms of my Starseed Self. I Am that I AM!

Day 28 I AM Spirit Giving Birth to Myself... I meditate, contemplating my own reflection of darkness and light... I AM the mystery of my soul's soil 'mystory'... I AM my journey. I AM that I AM gratitude and appreciation... I AM!

Day 0 I AM Spirit Giving Birth to Myself... I AM that I AM full moon womb Black wholeness... I AM that I AM Complete... Giving birth to my Starseed Self Anu... I AM fulfilling myself... I AM that I AM Selfull!!... I AM!

DEFINITIONS

(And their origins)

- Ahò - So it is/Thank you – (Lakota)
- Amen - So be it – (Christian/Hebrew/Khemetic)
- Ameen - So be it – (Islamic)
- Amom - So be it– (Nu Being Tribe Word Sound)
- Ani zay ani - I AM that I AM – (Aramaic)
- Anu -The royal child of Heaven. The God who leads the Soul to Rebirth (Kemetic Cosmology)
- Asè - So be it/Thank you – (Yoruba)
- Endarkening – When a person closes their eyes with conscious intent to explore their shadow side through meditation, revelation, and inspiration.Enlightenment through the death of the ego. (Tassili Ma'at)
- Gye Nyame - Akan Symbol/Ghana meaning "the Omnipotence of God" as well as "Fear none but God."
- In Lak'ech Ala K'in - I AM another yourself – (Ol'Mec/Mayan)
- Livity – A spiritual way of living (Rastafari Concept)
- Medasi ma nkwa - Giving thanks for life – (Twi)
- Namaste - I honor the place in you that is the same in me – (Sanskrit)
- Nuk Pu Nu - I AM that I AM – (Khemetic)
- Ori – Auric field/crown chakra
- Sat Nam - My name is Truth - (Sanskrit)
- Selfullness – It is a balanced love of self, state of being self-fulfilled (Tassili Ma'at)
- Ubuntu - I AM because we are, we are therefore I AM – (Zulu)
- Wholistic – (W)holistic with a "W" to experience wholeness (Tassili Ma'at)

Gye Nyame Symbol represents: "Fear none except for God"

Blackness... Consciousness...

DAY 0

When I close my eyes and go into what I call the Endarkening, I go all the way back to my first memory in this life. I remember 'nothing.' I mean the first thing I see is blackness. There is only a sense of feeling. And 'it' feels good. 'It' makes me smile. It's funny because I don't know what 'it' is. I just remember 'it.' And what is memory but the opportunity to connect that which is familiar. It's the mental action of putting back together pieces of ourselves, our lives. So, this memory of 'nothing,' the 'no thing'... Is just 'goodness.' I feel 'safe' and 'cared for.'

I have a sense of 'well-being.' Isn't that funny? I'm using all of these adjectives to describe 'nothing,' the 'no thing.' This unknown knowing of 'something.' The 'sum of things,' again which is of 'nothing,' which still existsbecause the feeling is still there. I mean I still feel 'it,' right now. And obviously, I don't know everything there is to know about 'it,' because I don'tknow what I don't know. But I AM thankful for what I do know. And I knowright now in this very moment... I feel good. Now, I'm tickled! Oh, wow! I'm smiling 'the inner smile.' Buddha's riddle comes to mind... "Is my smile the source of my joy, or is my joy the source of my smile?"

Is that the answer? I mean, I feel good! So, feeling good is the answer?!?
Remembering the 'nothing' which is 'something' that is 'good' and 'it's mine'
I have 'it' because 'it's' coming from 'my' memory of 'nothing'...
The blackness... The goodness... The cared for... The well-being... The smile...

The joy... 'It's' mine... It's me! I AM remembering "I AM that I AM..."

Deep...

So, what is your very first memory of this life? Was it a feeling for you too? All answers are valid. And if you don't remember, then just be still... 'Nothing' is present for you!

Affirmation... I AM Spirit Giving Birth to Myself... I AM that I AM!
Blackness...Consciousness... Before the Beginning... I AM!

In the Black Hole Moon Womb...

DAY 1

So the next question is: who am I? Right?!? So, I AM asking and answering the questions at the same time. LOL! Well, I don't really know in totality. I don't know who I AM in completion because my life isn't over yet. What I do know is what I experience in this moment. And then it becomes a memory because it is now the past. So does the past still exist? Seemingly no, not physically at least. I mean think about it. Now that the thought has been completed, it's done, gone into our memory bank. If we let it go, forget it, then it becomes a fragmented thought, buried in our subconscious mind. If we hold onto it, it becomes a strong part of our active consciousness. So, yes it still exists, it just changes form. Energy never really dies. Everything still exists in some way, even if just in our memory, our unconscious mind. It dwells in another dimension simultaneously as a part of the etheric realm. It's in what some call the Akasha/Akashic Records or the Collective Unconsciousness of the All that Is. Some call it the memory bank of Most High, the Hall of Records of the Divine Intelligence, The Dream Time.

Most ancient people have acknowledged this dimension as being a part of the creative life force that holds within it the collective vibrations of everything that ever was and ever will be. It is known as both our Heavenly Father and our Great Cosmic Mother. So, if the triple blackness of space is likened to the womb of the Great Cosmic Mother, then our soul matrix is the umbilicus that connects us to this dimension. And we are all connected to it via this silvery white ethereal cord. It connects to our crown chakra on one end and to the Akasha on the other. What is our soul matrix you ask? Well, in metaphysical terms, it is equivalent to an etheric computer printout of us. It is unique unto each creation and everything has one. Your next question might be, "How do

I know?" Well folks, this is one of those things that I just know that I know. It was what was revealed to me when I was still. Deep in meditation. Later in my spiritual studies it was verified by mystics much wiser than I AM.

This leads me to my next question. And so what about what I'm experiencing that I don't know that I don't know? I mean what caused the experience? Were others impacted in some way? I see this body. I hear me asking and answering these questions; but for real though. Who am I? And before that, what am I? I've been called a lot of things in my life occasionally some bad but mostly good like: girl, child, daughter, sister, woman, wife, mother, lover, teacher, chef, boss, entrepreneur, queen, empress. I've even been told that I AM made in the image and likeness of the divine... Goddess. What is certain is that I AM breathing, my heart is beating, and my body is functioning in a healthy way, as it should. I AM thinking and in this moment, writing. I AM alive. I was born out of my mother's womb and I AM here. I AM spirit. A spirit having a human experience....

A human, being. Who are you? What are you? In your original state of being, what do you remember? All answers are valid... Remember...

Affirmation... I AM Spirit Giving Birth to Myself... I AM that I AM in the Black Hole Moon Womb... I AM being!

Journey To Selfullness

In the beginning…

DAY 2

Well, as the story goes I was so comfy in my mother's womb, I didn't want to come out. So, I turned myself around. That's right, as a baby is preparing itself to be born, we all know it turns upside down to be pushed out head first. I chose to do the opposite; I went from being upside down to right side up on my predicted born day (due date). I was already beginning to determine my own way, co-creating my destiny. After being three days 'late,' my mom said the doctor and nurses decided to turn me around so that I wouldn't be born breached (feet first). Was this the beginning of my time management challenges?!? LOL! As a result of the pain from long hours of contractions, in the labor of love, my mother surrendered to the epidural.

There must've been something that caused me to try to 'breach those contracts' of life. When I try to remember, the only thing that comes to mind is that I wanted to stay close to my mom as long as I could. That must've been it, because we were never that close again. Even with me being born on her birthday, even with me being her gift. Now, don't get me wrong we were cool, but not as close as either of us would've liked. My mom said I never felt like I was hers. I belonged to everyone else. You know great grands, grands, aunts, uncles and cousins. They all took care of me. My lesson learned? Since the beginning I knew I was loved, yet I often felt disconnected and alone. So, I did my best to keep my own children close. I was creating a different reality.

Fast forwarding now to come 360°. I had a traumatic experience that I could not explain. Moments after I finished this book, 2 1/2 hours into my birthday 12/18/2019, I became terrified! I was in Belize staying in a cozy lodge in the jungle, at the top of the mountain. I felt safe, as I stayed there the night before with no problem. However, this night I became inexplicably fearful. I had gotten in the bed under the mosquito net and calmly said to myself "Ahhh, I'm in my mother's womb." Reminiscent of preparing to be born, I cuddled up into a fetal position. All of a sudden, I begin to go into a feeling of insecurity that quickly became anxiety. I've never experienced an anxiety attack, but from hearing about them that was the closest, if not it.

Anyway, no matter what I tried to do to calm myself, it just got worse. I went deep into prayer. There was nothing rational about it. I was so tired and yet my heart was racing, palpitating to a point that it hurt. I made myself go into deep breathing, until I finally just fell asleep. The next morning I was baffled. In meditation the only thing that came to me to explain it was that I was reliving the fear I had when the doctor came to turn me around. What was safe and cozy in my mother's womb had suddenly become unknown, unfamiliar, and scary! And I was alone, unprotected, and totally vulnerable. I had no control and thus became out of control, as they came for me. I fell asleep surrendering to the cellular memory of the epidural.

I had to include this new revelation in my birth story. It explains so many things in my life that I currently face and it's all valid because for better or worse it's all me. What is your birth story? What do you remember of your own birth? All answers are valid... So just remember....

Affirmation... I AM Spirit Giving Birth to Myself... In the beginning I AM creating... I AM!

____

____

____

____

____

____

____

Journey To Selfullness

I AM Creating 'creating'...

DAY 3

The doctor pulled me out. My head was pointed from the pressure of the forceps. I had a 'pyramid head' LOL. I AM legitimately a Unicorn! Fortunately the wisdom of my elders created a 'wizened dome' for me by reshaping my head. They massage my skull and made it perfectly round. While my soft spot gradually closed like normal babies, my ethereal crown chakra stayed open. The trauma of the forceps created the necessary pressure to activate my crown chakra. Thus my pituitary and pineal glands were activated. So, I was very psychically sensitive from birth. How else could it be explained, as no one said I was born with 'a veil,' which is usually the way a psychically sensitive is born. This inner light made it so that I had very vivid and sometimes prophetic dreams. I could 'see beyond sight.' My way of saying I could see spirits.

I could also hear and feel them, too. And sometimes I just knew certain things and I couldn't explain it, I just knew that I knew. All of this was going on at a very early age. As far back as I can remember, and still to this day, when I close my eyes and go into the Endarkening, at first there is only blackness. Then there is light. I AM seeing lights and patterns. A kaleidoscope of colors and then forms. Visions of people, places and things, known and unknown come to me. So out of the trauma of life, I was given a gift. I use it to be of service, to assist others in remembering what they really already know.

I've learned to accept this about myself as the part of me that connects me directly to my divinity, my higher Self! What gifts were you born with? How have you use them? Is there something unique, different, strange, or weird, about you that helps you to be connected to your higher self? Remember all answers are valid.

Affirmation...I AM Spirit Giving Birth to Myself... I AM Creating "creating" ... I go into the Endarkening...There IS light... I AM.

DAY 4

Being a psychically sensitive child wasn't easy. In fact, it was scary a lot of the time. No one believed me when I told them I saw a man standing in the room or saw faces of people next to the fireplace. I had no proof as no one else in my family said they could see them. I was told "there's no such thing as ghosts," "girl, you're crazy," "there's no one there." "Stop saying that!" So, I was afraid and felt alone at times. I didn't know why I knew certain things before they happen. I just knew. Déjà vu was a close companion. I didn't understand why I was drawn to mythology, mystery stories, and then later it became the mystical. Looking back, it was a path that was created for me by my higher Self, my spirit guides and my ancestors. But then, all I knew was that I loved those topics, the books, movies, the information, and games.

I loved spooky campfire stories and songs. I even loved Halloween haunted houses, as long as they weren't too scary! At age 10, I started participating in slumber party séances with friends. No one ever actually was 'as light as a feather' so we never got to really levitate anyone. I do remember living for the thrill and excitement of exploring the unknown as a group. I had segments of visions all the time; however, I remember the first complete vision I had was when I was eight years old.

Spirit showed me the origin of albinos. This later led me on a journey to discover some the secrets of evolution and the karma of why some things are as they are.... (A sharing for my next book LOL). However at the time, I got such mixed responses from the adults when I shared what I saw in the vision, that I just let it go. The Ouija board was more fascinating to me. So, I asked for one and got it for Christmas. I eagerly asked a 100 questions and got some accurate answers. Then one day a classmate of mine said, "The Ouija board is run by the devil!" So, when I got home I asked the Ouija board, "Was it run by the devil?" And it responded, "Yes." So, I promptly put it back in its box and threw it in the trash can. My mom saw it in there the next morning and asked why it was there? I told her I didn't want anything to do with the devil. I chose between what I knew to be good and bad, between live and evil. At the time, I didn't know the 'word sound power remix' of the words 'evil' and 'live' as well as the 'devil' and 'lived.'

Later spirit showed me that 'devil' is 'lived' backward and it describes someone who has lived in discord with universal law and continues to live in a backward, disconnected negative way. And as I said earlier 'evil' is just 'live' backwards. Someone who lives in a backwards or contrary way to that which promotes life for the good of the whole. It wasn't a man with horns and a pitchfork.

I was being tested by the universe/God/my higher Self. Somehow... I knew enough to know what I AM being and what I AM not... It's innate. And by the way the Ouija board in and of itself is not evil. However, it can attract and channel some lower vibrational entities. I would advise to use it with caution.

What are some words that you remixed, heard of, or used? What childhood test did you have and what did you choose and why? Remember all answers are valid and no one will see this unless you show them.

Affirmation... I AM Spirit Giving Birth to Myself... I AM the Endarkening... I AM the light... I AM that I AM... I AM that I AM Being and I AM that I AM Not!

____

____

____

____

Journey To Selfullness

Journey To Selfullness

Awareness... I Will willingly...

DAY 5

So, what is it in us that makes us do what we do and not do what we don't do? I mean, I chose based on that which made me feel better, certain, secure, and good. Usually it's a small voice within us that tells us the right or best thing to do. That along with the feeling of the right or best choice, you'd think it would be easy to just do the right thing. But as humans, being, we get the opportunity to exercise free will. And what is that you say?

Well, it's the time to be in discovery of possibilities! What a thrill! Then we choose to not always listen to that small voice. We choose the opposite. And then when things don't go the way we wanted or thought it would, we say "something" told me not to do that, but I didn't listen. Now, I'm in trouble or I've got a mess or a problem to deal with. I knew I should've listened! Rev. Dr. Barbara King said, "Something" is one of the more common names for God. It's that 'something' that is 'nothing' that is always with us, always giving us that familiar Black, that not knowing of certainty.

In modern times, Blackness has become associated with fear, terror, and danger. Yet for all life, the night is certain and necessary. Darkness must and always comes. Closing your eyes 'it' is there. It's the process of Endarkening. For indigenous people and enslaved Africans the night time meant freedom. It meant safety. It was a sacred time for Spirit to come and communicate in the dreamtime. Darkness, the Blackness, is the only constant. Before there was light there was only the blackness. All scriptures and sacred text speak of it - before beginningless time. All scriptures and sacred text say in some form or another that, "We are made in the image and likeness of the Divine" and "To be still and know that I AM God."

Blackness is still the 'stillness.' So, will you willingly be still? Will you explore the darkness? What will you choose to make known? Will you choose to discover what you don't know? Will you explore the Endarkening and experience yourself as the 'stillness?' Will you make known the unknown? Or do you choose to be in fear (false evidence appearing real…)? What will you explore as reality and about yourself? So, what does that make you? What will you choose? Will you choose to discover what you don't know, you don't know? Will you choose to know who/what you are? Who or what will you create, as yourself, to be?

Affirmation… I AM Spirit Giving Birth to Myself… Awareness… I Will willingly… I AM that I AM… The Self of my Self's creation… I AM!

Journey To Selfullness

I AM light... I AM the star...

DAY 6

Ahhh, and now you see, you've got the power to choose what you want to be based on what you are discovering about yourself! So going into the darkness, you begin to see some light. It's the Endarkening. So, close your eyes again... this time notice the sparks of light - the twinges of patterns, kaleidoscopes of color, or maybe still the blackness. If you only see black, then look at something from your memory. Say, for example, a frog. Do you see the frog from your memory? If you still don't see it, get a picture of a frog, and stare at it. Now close your eyes and remember the picture of it. Do that regularly until you begin to see things automatically with your eyes closed. That is one way to develop your 'first eye' muscle, your pituitary gland. You are beginning to train yourself to 'see beyond sight.' You are becoming aware of illumination from within. You have always been a self-generated light. You are your own starlight discovering yourself out of the darkness! It's the Endarkening.

I became aware of my own light quite by surprise. As a single mom, self-employed, working from home, raising my children, there were times I felt like crap! And because I felt like crap, I thought I look like crap too! On some of those days, I wanted to crawl under a rock or go in a cave and hide. Sometimes it was all I could do to keep it moving. I had to, there was no one else to do it. Anyway, I'd go out to handle my business and people would stop me and say how great I looked. Or that I had a glow. Sometimes they even said I was radiant! I would be soooo confused! I knew they had to be talking to someone else, not me because I looked and felt like crap! And yet there was no one else around. They were absolutely talking to me! It took a while for me to get it. But finally I did. The 'glow,' the 'looking good,' the 'radiant,' had to be coming from within me. Fortunately, everyone else could see it, even though I couldn't. My higher Self, the Divine Intelligence, within me was showing through illuminating me. I begin to realize that I was onto 'something.' That 'something' was shifting within me. So, I continued to meditate and do my yoga. These key activities were helping me to cultivate my inner light. I was becoming aware of my star seeds self! Do you desire the cultivation of your sixth sense? If so, what activities do you do to enhance your psychic sensitivity? Are you willing to research, explore, and discover?

Affirmation… I AM Spirit Giving Birth to Myself… I AM light… I AM the Star… I AM the Seed of Being… I AM!

Journey To Selfullness

I AM the Blackness... I AM the Dark Matter...

DAY 7

I begin doing yoga at age 17. My first teacher was a man named Jomo. He was an inmate at Tennessee State Penitentiary serving a life sentence for murder. I met him in the projects at an after-school program. It was sponsored by a community agency called NATE. I don't remember what the acronym stood for, but it united model prisoners with the community in service. These model prisoners were scheduled to be released in four months. I was fortunate enough to be able to work with them for two months before my freshman year at Fisk University was about to break for the summer. Brother Jomo and I hit it off right away. I asked him to tell me his story. What happened, what went wrong? Brother Jomo had come home from work early and found his wife in bed with another man. He went to the kitchen and got his gun. He shot and killed his wife and wounded her lover. The jury found him guilty of premeditated manslaughter rather than a crime of passion because they said he had time to think when he went into the kitchen. Although he was sentenced for life, he was being released after 10 years.

Brother Jomo attributed his freedom to yoga and meditation. After being on lockdown for a month, he was in the library and found a book on yoga. After reading it for one week he asked to be placed in solitary confinement to practice his yoga and meditation. He was granted this request. Brother Jomo had no prior offenses and, in fact, he was one of the most kind and gentle people you'd ever meet. His captors began to recognize this in his character. As he cultivated himself, of course, his discipline grew. He envisioned himself a free man. He began to be of service by first working in the laundry facility, then he went on to other jobs until he got his first parole hearing. 10 years later, Brother Jomo was granted his freedom. His story moved me so that I began to study yoga from him. This practice shaped the foundation of my life. Through yoga, I began to cultivate my shine, even though I didn't know it yet. All I did know was that this humble man created his freedom, his reality by practicing yoga. In the darkness of the unknown, he inquired of the Divine Intelligence to show him how to be free. In the Endarkening, he was still enough to listen, to seek, to find, to study, to practice, to do, and to be... Free. The Divine Intelligence is always in all ways speaking to us. That small quiet voice, that is 'something' that is 'nothing' is always in all ways guiding us, if we but listen. If we are still... in discovery of ourselves, our own light, our own shine, will guide us.

What story or person do you know who has triumphed over despair? How did they find their light in the darkness of their soul? How has it helped or inspired you?

Affirmation... I AM Spirit Giving Birth to Myself... I AM the Blackness... I AM the Dark Matter Soil of my Soul in which I plant the Starseed of myself... I AM!

Journey To Selfullness

Tassili Ma'at is pictured here at the opening of the Natural Mystic Fair while honoring the ancestors during the Libations at The Cascade Nature Park in Atlanta, GA, 2017.

I AM the movement...

DAY 8

My spiritual journey continued as I experience the art of family. There comes a time when it is time to give birth. Whether it's a physical child or a project child. For me birthing a physical child came at the right time, for it set the course of my life. One of the greatest and most empowering thing a woman or a man can do is give birth. Of course, it's different for women and men. In most ideal circumstances it goes something like this. For men to give birth, according to the men I've asked, it's nothing short of a miracle. He puts himself into a woman's yoni/vagina and ideally shares immense pleasure, culminating in orgasms giving a portion of his life force to her. She absorbs it and transforms it. And nine months later he has an extension of himself. If he as the father is present in all ways as his gift to his spirit child's life, he will continue to nurture the Starseed that is the spirit child transforming.

He, as the father, will continue to fertilize ethereally with his thoughts, his words, and his deeds unto the mother/Earth as she incubates their Starseed creation. He, as father, is sometimes moved to tears that become the sacred libation as their Starseed shape shifts through the portal to the dimension that is Life, taking its first human breath. He as father receives and holds, welcoming this new Starseed sojourner into this third dimensional realm.

Again, in ideal circumstances, it goes something like this. For a woman she receives the man's lingam/phallus and life force elixir/spermand takes it in. She keeps it and creates a miracle. By combining his life force with hers, his sperm fertilizes her egg and transforms everything in her wholeworld forever. She becomes a shape shifter and the space within her space begins to move. Life is felt as she is feeling. There is the external shift as a result of the internal shift. Everything is new as Creation is creating itself. There is only surrender to the process of life begetting itself. It is the most ancient of rituals. As a mother, she is fully present for everything, always in all ways. She is in discovery as the process unfolds itself. Moving to its own rhythm and flow, a heartbeat is but a heartbeat away as she places her handson the orb that is the temporary home of the spirit child. Swimming in the waters of life, we are born again through our progeny, our children.

We give birth to ourselves by extending life through them. Ankh. Six times, I gave birth. Only five spirit children stayed. Each one, special unto themselves. Each contraction, a labor of love. Each contraction, revealing a purpose, 'Nia.' Each one, my favorite. My first child is my favorite because he set the foundation for my life. He will always be my firstborn, always leading the way. My second is my favorite because he is my miracle child. One of the twins, he was born early at seven months, weighing in at 1 lb. 14 oz., hardly expected to live. Not only did he survive to this day, he still thrives. My third is my favorite because he is just "easy." Never a problem for his self or anyone else. His life has been beauty and grace for all like his name. My fourth is my favorite because he is the one hoped and prayed for. He was the only one planned. And he is my last baby boy. My fifth child is my favorite because she is my only daughter. She is the baby and my gift for a job well done in birthing her brothers.

It is the only life relationship that can never be denied... The miracle of one's own life and the life that is created from two lives alchemically blending. It is the way, the continuum of life's must need for itself. Birthing itself from the vast ocean of consciousness.

What do you know of childbirth? Have you been pregnant? Have you ever sired a child? Have you been around anyone who has? Maybe your birth experience was not so idyllic. Maybe you miscarried, maybe you aborted? There is no judgment to you, only you and your quietude. There is the spiritual experience and then there is the actual physical experience. Sometimes they are vastly different. Either way both are valid... Please give birth to your truth.If these memories are too painful to explore alone, please seek counseling. It is time to heal.

Affirmation... I AM Spirit Giving Birth to Myself... I AM the Movement that is the wave of the dark waters of Cosmic Womb Ocean... I AM the sacred waters of life saturating my Starseed Self... I AM!

Journey To Selfullness

DAY 9

The 'project child' was birthed not too long after, as I had to work. My project child was becoming 'self-employed.' I figured it out based on what worked and what didn't. My 'wasbeen' and I were young and new to taking care of ourselves. We went straight from college into a marriage and family. Of course, he worked outside the home. Then I got a job outside the home, too. I make the distinction because often times working at home or being a homemaker is overlooked as not being 'work' or not being a 'real job.' I'm sure many readers can relate on some level. There is a big difference in sitting at home on your butt and being at home engaged in your children, home maintenance, food preparation, and running a business. In fact, in many ways it's even more work because it never stops. It just continues to ebb and flow. The seasons come and go and come again. In the season after my second pregnancy, I went to work outside the home again. This time with two children in day care.

I received an advance for my first week's pay. I actually was supposed to have a week in the hole (hmmmmm... a weak place in a hole, meant the sidesof the hole inevitably would collapse and bury me!) Now I know you're sayingwhere did that come from? I'll tell you... I used word sound power or gematria... The remixing of words or the discovery of the hidden meaning of words that keep magic spells going. That's why it's called 'spelling' when writing a word or speaking (spelling out loud) it into creation. I was about to be caught in the 'employment trap.' That's right, only making enough to take care of barely enough so that I can keep the cycle going and never be able to break it. Let me explain further what that looks like. After receiving my pay of $200 and then paying for childcare, I had only $20 left! So, essentially I wasworking to pay someone else to raise my children! Oh hell no! It wasn't even enough to contribute to any of the other bills, which was the point of me going to work in the first place.

So, I quickly stopped that madness by quitting my job. The reality was, however, that I still needed to work. So I just started braiding hair for a living. It just so happened that at the time designer braids and fancy beadwork were becoming quite popular. With encouragement from my friends, I began to charge for my hair braiding skills. My 'wasbeen' was upset because he wanted a corporate woman as his wife. I was never that... Until now LOL, but now it's on my own terms. My entrepreneurial life was real legit self-employment. Even though for 35 years, my dad kept asking, "When are you going to get areal job?" LOL! My friends would make careless remarks that I was at home doing nothing... (Mind you at the time none of them were married nor had children.)

It takes a lot to keep going forward when everyone tells you you're wrong. My parents used to tell me I was wasting my brain. All because I chose to stay home and raise my children and work. My braiding business was steady and so I was able to help pay the bills in spite of my wasbeen's complaints. As my children got older, our house became the kids hang out. Every day the neighborhood children gathered at our home to play. I treated all the children like my own and they loved it. So did their parents. It was soon apparent that I needed to start charging for that too! So my childcare business was born.

I loved working for myself. Even if others didn't value it, my children and the parents of their friends did. The children loved being with me and I was 'the neighborhood mom.' Yep, even then I was 'Mama Tassili.' But, sometimes I felt really sad and all alone. Sometimes I felt like I didn't belong, like what I was doing just didn't matter. It was like no matter what I did, it was never enough. Have you ever felt like that? Like what you were doing didn't matter? Deep down inside you knew it did, but no one else recognized it. Yet, you didn't quit. When did this happen for you?

Affirmation... I AM Spirit Giving Birth to Myself... I Am Reverberations of eb and flow... I create the warmth of the heat I Am...I AM nurturing my Starseed Self in the Soul of my Soul... I AM!

DAY 10

Becoming an adult, as a young woman was hard at times. My time was really never my own anymore. Between mothering, wifing, working, and homemaking, there was no time for me. Most of the time I felt empty, except for the fulfillment from raising my children and the reward from my work. My wasbeen wasn't happy with me nor I with him. We were married in the mid-70s and couples were, for the most part, still expected to stay together no matter what. I didn't know myself. My first attempt at self-discovery was to meditate on the name that my parents had given me. It was Sheryl Lynn Williams. I never liked it. Ever since I could remember it never seemed to fit me!It felt like it didn't belong to me. And by the way, I felt like I didn't really belong to my family either. I mean, I know I wasn't adopted, because everyone always said I look like my mom. But I couldn't see it.

I wanted to look like myself. Looking back I realize, I was kind of angry with my mom a lot of the time, so I was indifferent towards her. As I'm writing this, I'm reminded of the ridiculousness of my three year old self totally dismissing my mother because she, in my three-year-old mind left me to go visit my dad. All those years I held that against her. She didn't even know. And how could she? It wasn't until recently that I realized that that's what was going on with me. SMH... please forgive me, Mama! Anyway, back to myname. I didn't like my name especially when I was in trouble and it seemed like I was always in trouble. My parents, elders, teachers, and other miscellaneous adults would always say my whole name! That's how I knew I was in trouble!

As soon as I was aware enough, I was thinking of a nickname. In the fifth grade, I thought about "Snoopy" as a possibility because everybody liked Snoopy on The Charlie Brown TV special. So it seemed like a good choice.
I told a friend, she frowned and said "Ewww! That's a dog's name and you're

not a dog!" I never got to explain why I liked it. It was immediately 'thrown to the dogs!' Pun intended LOL! My next attempt stuck for a while. It was Tamu, Kiswahili for 'sweet.' At age 14, I begin to take art seriously. I drew constantly, almost as much as I read books. When I went to sign my artwork the name Sheryl just never seem to fit. It didn't even look right at the bottom of the picture. Neither did my initials. So I chose the first African name I learned. I mean that I actually knew what it meant and where it was from. During those years, black folks were trying to decide who we were. Were we Negroes, black, African, colored, African-American, Africans in America. What were we? Who were we?

My mom was a community activist. So we, mostly me, because my brothers were just so young, were exposed to a lot of the community organizations and ideologies. One of them being the US organization and their leader, Dr. Maulana Karenga. Thus my exposure to Kwanzaa. I started participating in Kwanzaa activities at age 12. I had learned that we were supposed to practice the seven principles of Kwanzaa, 365 days a year. So, Kujichaguli– self-determination gave me the right to define for myself, name myself, teach myself, govern myself, defend myself, etc. I got it! So I became Tamu on all of my creative works. Later at Fisk University when I was 18 I met the Ajanaku family. They added to my growing knowledge of self as an African in America. They embraced me and I embraced them. So I became Tamu Ajanaku. "Ajanaku" meant "the fight for the liberation of African people till death." So I begin to embody "the sweet fight for the liberation of African people until death." My pan African experience grew into a spiritual quest.

Still 18 and beginning my sophomore year, I took my "Shahadah" and embraced Islam. The "Shahadah" is the bearing witness that "there is no God but Allah and that the Prophet Mohammed is his servant and apostle." And of course, I received a new name for this season of my journey. My Islamic name was Yasmin Amatula Waduda. Which means "Jasmine flower, the servant of the loving attribute of Allah." Some called me Tamu Ajanaku, while others called me Yasmin and when I went home, my family still called me Sheryl. And there was still the whole thing that would happen when I was in trouble. So, of course, I was in big trouble when I came home with my whole head shaved bald, as Tamu Ajanaku.

My being in trouble continued when I came home for Xmas break pregnant and unwilling to be married! Lol - smh! My "wasbeen" wanted to marry me when I first became pregnant. It was the honorable thing to do. I didn't want to get married just because I was pregnant. He had already asked me to marry him a couple of months earlier. I said yes, but wanted to live together a couple years first to see if we could even do it. I held out for several and then I went on and got married to him in the seventh month of pregnancy.I became Sheryl Lynn Williams-Knight. So on my 20th birthday, I stayed homeand meditated on who and what I had become. I had just gotten married andhad a baby. I was also considered a "woman." With no formal rite of passage,I was in a state of discovery about all that I didn't know that I didn't know. All three of those states of being were unfolding simultaneously all the time. The only thing certain I knew that I hadn't changed about me was my birth name...Sheryl Lynn Williams. So I begin to focus on that. I had to take a new look at it and find out what did it really mean, since it was all I really had that was "mine."

So using word sound power, I saw that "Sheryl" was really "She is real." Also "She of Israel." It is also the name of a small white flower pronounced "Chervil," that grows in the meadows of England. It is an herb used for digestion and flavor. It was derived from "Shirley" which was a surname (last name) at one time. By the way, that was my mother's first name. I wonder if she knew.

"Lynn" came from the Asian goddess, "Quan Lin" she's most commonly known as "Kwan Yen." The mythologies speak of her as "The Divine Mother" and the "Goddess of Prosperity," "Williams" was derived from "William's son." And "William" came from "William the Conqueror," King of England, a warrior King.

Using words sound power, I realized it also meant "Will I AM."

All of a sudden, Sheryl Lynn Williams wasn't so bad. To top it off, the new addition of "Knight" was also clearly a warrior name. Even though none of them were African, I liked the meanings nonetheless. They were all of a similar or same frequency. Especially "Ajanaku" and the other warrior names. Inhaling and exhaling deeply, I smiled discovering a new sense of self. What/when was your first sense of yourself? Did your birth name or any other names help you to discover you in anyway? Remember all answers are valid!

Affirmation... I AM Spirit Giving Birth to Myself... I AM that I AM Cultivating "cultivating" my Starseed Self..." I AM!

Journey To Selfullness

Journey To Selfullness

DAY 11

In the early years of my life as a mother, wife, entrepreneur, and homemaker, I was lost. There were flickers of my light, my soul shine, but they were few and far in between. I was overwhelmed, undervalued and by today's standards, somewhat depressed. However, back in the day, we didn't have the luxury of being bipolar or unbalanced. In fact, mental health, or mental illness wasn't even a 'real' topic in the black community. No one talked about it. We just had to figure it out. So, I did. When my "wasbeen" and I were dating, we promised to be vegetarian when we got married. He changed his mind and refused to take it on. So after a couple of months I started eating fish and chicken again. Before getting married, I had become a vegetarian because I didn't like the mis-treatment of the animals. So, compassion was my reason for conversion. I later learned the health and spiritual benefits. In my second semester of my sophomore year at Fisk, I read up on everything I could find.

I wanted my baby and future children to have the best life had to offer. "Back to Eden" by Jethro Kloss, "Cooking with Mother Nature" by Dick Gregory and Survival Into the 21st Century - Planetary Healer's Manual" by Victoras Kulvinskas, MS, were my Bibles on Health. Once married, I made everything from scratch and learned all about herbs. I grew in knowledge and experience. It was a house divided, the more I learned about health and well-being, the more my "wasbeen" rebelled and ate worse. The more African centered I became the more Euro centered he became.

Even spirituality became a battleground. It wasn't so much that he wanted me to be a particular faith. He just didn't support me in being Muslim. The more metaphysical I became, the more mainstream and conformity appealed to him. The one thing he did support me in though was my name change. He was the only family member that I invited that showed up.

After reading the book, "The Oldest Africans," I was drawn to the name Tassili. It really resonated with me. The book showed pictures of cave paintings and rock carvings over 50,000 years old in a mountainous region in the south eastern part of Algeria known as Tassili Niger. The book spoke of the rocks and mountains being "record keepers." Pictographs of a time found only in the depths of our ancestral memory. There were/are even glyphs of the 'Star People,' our galactic ancestors. I begin to embrace myself as an artist again, "one who is keeper of the records thru the arts" and so in the spirit of Kujichagulia, "Tassili" became my newest name.

I had a traditional West African naming ceremony performed by a Serer (A tribe in the region of Senegal) Priest/Imam, Zack Diouf. Baba Zack performed the ceremony and he said that "Tassili" had an Islamic root, "Tashree." The "ree" was pronounced like a "D." Baba Zach said it was the name of one of the mountains Moshe (Moses) went to for one of his initiations. So, it also meant "high spiritual attainment." A year later I met a man from Algeria who told me the modern day meaning is "the heights," "the highest standard and finest quality." In doing some research in African history, I later found out its most ancient root is derived from the Ta Seti people of ancient Kemet. The people of "the Bow" (as in bow and arrow). They were the ones that learned from the Twa people. "Bes" is depicted as their very first teacher.

They built the most ancient of the Kemetic civilizations at the birth of the Nile, upper Egypt/Kemet. They were also known as the people of Meroë and were ruled by the Kandakè Queens. Queen Hatshepsut was of this lineage. The Ta Seti people migrated all over the continent leaving cave paintings and rock carvings as proof of their presence. I was growing and beginning to know me. On some levels this was crazy in the making! As an artist not able to make time to fully express herself, I still had to create or lose my mind! So I became my canvas. I became a living sculpture of mixed media expression. I expressed my *Africanity* with my baldhead (1975 to 1987), African and ethnic clothing and jewelry! In what ways have you had to create yourself "a way out of noway" to maintain your sanity? How many names have you had? Have you explored their meanings? What fills your passion?

Affirmation...I AM Spirit Giving Birth to Myself... I AM that I AM formulation of my Starseed Self...I AM!

Journey To Selfullness

DAY 12

At this point, it was clear that my "wasbeen" and I were on two diverging paths; never to be parallel much less intertwined again. I begin to take charge of my time. First by embracing my sacred moon time. My "wasbeen" was the type of man that wanted sex pretty much every night. I would've had no problem with that, however, he like most modern men had no training or discipline in holding his seed. So consequently the sex was over in 10 to 15 minutes. Leaving him spent and me unfulfilled. That became extremely frustrating.

The things we did before getting married, he didn't want to do after marriage. So our sex life was no fun and pretty passionless. In fact, he had multiple affairs. I had been told by the older women in my family that I should never talk to my family or friends about my personal business. They said I should just pray about it. I didn't know what to do. So there were all kinds of imbalances for all kinds of reasons. He also smoked cigarettes, herb, and drank beer usually in between coming home from work and going to bed. So his breath wasn't appealing either. I was also taught that you never turn your husband down when he wants sex, otherwise he'll go elsewhere. LOL! I didn't turn him down and yet he went elsewhere anyway!

So, so much for that bit of advice. Now I wasn't fat, did my Kagle's and kept up my body and my hygiene. So I'll never know what was really up, maybe we just weren't compatible. Maybe we just came together to have our three wonderful sons. Who knows?!? I seriously doubt if he even knew. (He actually admitted that later.) We simply grew apart. Couples and singles, if you want to stay together, please take heed... This info could really help you, if you are both honest. Anyway, I just knew I needed a reprieve from wifely duties. So

I told him I didn't want to have sex during my moon cycle. He agreed.

It really wasn't a problem for me in general, because I loved having sex then and now. I just needed to know I could have a designated time for myself. It was perfect. I still cooked cleaned and worked. I just didn't have to have sex for a week. Instead I used that time as my "me time." It became my sacred bath time. I would take baths in milk and honey, oils, and herbs. I wrote poetry and sometimes even made jewelry. I began to love the darkness and lit candles and incense to bless the space.

I began to have the most vivid visions and meditations. My word sound remix of my name became Tassili Night (well not officially until we divorced). My cycle would come with every new moon and I'd ovulate in the full moon. After my third pregnancy, my cycle begin to alternate with the equinox and solstice. My cycle synchronized alternately by sometimes ovulating with the new moon and flowing with the full moon. My Moon time became my best friend not only because it meant I wasn't pregnant but also because it was my sacred time to be with me.

What was your definitive moment for you? When did you say I need this time for me? Or have you acknowledged it yet?

Affirmation… I AM Spirit Giving Birth to Myself… I AM that I AM pushing through my Soul's Soil… Taking the form of that which is in formation… My Starseed Self fills with expansion… I AM!

____

____

____

____

Journey To Selfullness

DAY 13

I met my first spiritual teacher, Marva Moore, at age 25. At this point I had had three children and was anxiously birthing myself! Marva was introduced to me at a time when my questions about Life had deepened. They say "when the student is ready the teacher appears" and so it was. My studies of secret/sacred signs, symbols and sigils had activated my ancestral memoryin every way. I was committed to my souls' evolution... to ascension. Marva taught metaphysics and magic, Goddess/God consciousness, wise woman ways, and ancestral connections.

I learned about chakras, and received Shaktipat's initiation from my second Spiritual teacher, Dr. Sherifa Saa. She activated my chakras to a higher frequency and then tweaked that! (I am shivering). She taught rituals, energy healing, chakra balancing, color science, levitation and more. The yearning for seeking grew even more. And "Yemaya" called. I was beckoned to 'Voyage'... songstress Angela Bofill's dedication to "Yemaya," IFA Goddess of the Sea and my first Orisha. I was possessed by this Sea Goddess, Divine Mother of Abundance.

Powerful and mysterious... I searched to know who she was. In my seeking, I found her deeply rooted in African Cosmology. She was the first, The Great Cosmic Mother, The Triple Blackness of Space. In her womb, the heavens swim. She gives birth to all and in the end, all must return to her. She is known by many names throughout the world, throughout all cultures, throughout all time. I learned that IFA came from Old Yorubaland and survived through the diaspora. It was preserved as Macumba and Candomblè by way of Brazil. Yemaya's possessions of me showed up in the form of trance dance. I was compelled daily, a minimum of five times a day, to dance with/for her.

Alone or in the midst of a crowd, it didn't matter. When the energy came over me, I was not 'just' myself. I became more. It felt like I became her. My initiation was coming from the inner plains. I was on a relentless scavenger hunt. Seeking, searching to find whatever I could that would feed this burning desire to know, to connect, to be complete, to be whole. Making known the unknown, while knowing that I didn't know what I didn't know. Yet, I knew I was being guided to learn to acknowledge what I knew that I knew but didn't know how I knew.

I was mysteriously gifted some 'elekes' (Orisha beads) without even knowing what they were at first. Then meeting Ye Ye Louisa Tiesh, now an Ifaniya (High Priestess) was everything! She, who told me of IFA, read me and said that "They all want me." "The Orisha would take their turns with me" and that they have! And ultimately, that it was still not my time to be formally initiated in IFA. She said I had more seeking to do. Marva Moore had created a metaphysical group called the Institute of African Mysticism. We traveled throughout Mexico and visited the temples and pyramids of the Olmec-Mayan and other richly Melanated people who called themselves by their own ancient names. They spoke about our ancestors who came from the heavens and were called the Star People. These indigenous ones of these western shores called us "Starseeds." My shine grows! I know of who I AM! I AM bright, I AM adaughter of the triple blackness of the night. I AM luminous. I AM the light. I AM full with the knowledge of my ancient indigenous self.

Who do you knowyourself to be as your most ancient Self? What inner plain initiations did you have? It's okay to remember. You're in a safe place now. Remember all answers are valid.

Affirmation... I AM Spirit Giving Birth to Myself... I AM that I AM that I AM Starseed of myself actualizing fullness... I AM!

I AM that I AM the Starseed of myself born again...

DAY 14

I AM called in many directions. The seven-year cycle of my marriage season was over. My "wasbeen" and I had gone our separate ways. What to do with myself and my three rambunctious sons? Back to school, down to Mexico, to my inner sanctum of creativity, to the Akashic records of The Knowing. I AM called to shine. Newly divorced I enrolled back in school at The University of California at San Diego. It had been seven years since I had been in college. So I had to start all over again. I began with art courses. So, of course I did well! I got all A's! That was really empowering! And I loved it! I was so full!

Totally Selfull! I found meaning and purpose for me. It was great to be a mom, though single, parenting was hard. Dating was fun, but disappointing as well. With my family's help, I managed my life. Although most of the time was taken up with my boys and being present in their lives. Things balanced out. Ilearned massage and became a massage therapist. So, still entrepreneurial, I worked at a spa, braided hair, went to school and created art. I still looked forward to my sacred moon time. It was then that I became more involved with wise women's witchy ways that were sacred unto nature's wild women who dance with wolves, horses, unicorns and dragons... All my ancestors loved me and treated me well. They knew I loved them more and more every day in every way.

For clarity's sake for the readers who are a little leery... This may be your first time being exposed to this kind of information and I want you to be clear about where I stand with the forces of good and evil. I must let you know I have never used any prayer, incantation, or spell for anything negative. I have not done anything to go against another person's will in any way. I have sworn never to do harm intentionally directly or indirectly. I have used the sacred sciences only and always in all ways for the highest good of all. That having been said I'll continue sharing my journey to Selfullness! I was gifted a book called "The Bible and the Tarot." I was gifted a Tarot deck as well. I began playing with the cards and soon learned to read them according to the book.

This was right before backpacking down to central Mexico with my three young sons for the summer. We went to stay in a small mountain town called San Miguel de Allande in the state of Guanajuato. We took a train, a bus and taxis to get there. Everywhere on the road, I was continually asked to 'read' for people. OMG! I was barely 'reading' for myself, how could I 'read' for others? And how did they know?!? It was as if I had a sign on my back that said "Divina" (Spanish for diviner, reader). I kept telling people "no," but they just kept asking. I can only say they saw my light and I looked like a gypsy. I was still bald, but wore a scarf when traveling. And I wore skirts and dresses all the time, never pants. Wow! Reflecting on that I didn't wear pants for 20 years.

The closest thing that came to that would be when I wore harem pants or Hausa pants (MC Hammer pants). Spirit told me I had to keep my energy flowing. I had to stay connected from my crown chakra receiving heavenly emanations thru to my root chakra, receiving the earth elemental essence. I was guided to do that in 1984 on my journey to the pyramids in Mexico with the Institute of African Mysticism. I continued that practice until 2004. Spirit said I had to learn to master the feminine portals as women are open on both ends. Little did I know that I was being prepped for channeling? Anyway we stopped for the night in a little town called Copalio. The receptionist at the Inn where we stayed asked me at least five times to 'read' for her, before I finally said "Okay, I'll pray about it."

So I did a reading on it. And the reading was favorable. So I prayed that if they, The Most High and my Spirit Guides, wanted me to do this then please speak through me. I knew I didn't know what I was doing and I never wanted to hurt or mislead anyone. I asked that if I had a gift, that it would be taken away if I were to ever go astray. Anyway, I was guided to bless the room. When the receptionist came up, I said a prayer. It was very simple because I didn't know Spanish that well. I was fluent enough to get around, but not to do a reading! So it was to my surprise that I spoke Spanish well enough and more thoroughly than I ever had. I knew The Most High, the Holy Spirit was speaking through me. The receptionist was so pleased she went and got two of her cousins so they could get readings.

I refuse to take money, because I had heard tales of Mexican prisons without roofs. And I didn't wanna take a chance of endangering my sons or myself. I never wanted to be accused of being a charlatan, false prophetess, crook or anything of that sort. So my rationale was if I didn't take any money they couldn't arrest me if something went wrong. I told them they could simply pay me with food. So the receptionist and her cousins took us out to dinner. When we arrived in San Miguel, it was the same thing. People continued to seek me for counseling. I refused to take money. I fed us that entire month; my sons were with me while doing readings. Amazing it was! I found my calling and although I was still growing in it, I felt really great that I was being of service. My sons were happy from the experience we had had in Mexico. My brother came and got them and when they left, I was on my own. One day, I traveled with a woman to a remote village outside of San Miguel. The countryside was covered with small pyramids. Who knew pyramids were all over Mexico, not just on the Gulf.

They reminded me of the small pyramids of ancient Meroe along the Nile, built by the Ta Seti people. Entering her village was like going back in time. The huts were made of clay and the roofs were either corrugated iron or thatched straw. I saw no one outside walking around when we entered her hut. I 'read' for her and her sister. She gave me a bag of potatoes as my payment and we prepared to leave. When I came outside her door, there wereat least 50 people waiting to see me and or touch me! Scary! OMG! I wasn't ready for that. I could feel the local Bruja's (witch) eyes on me, yet I didn't see her physically. No, I felt her eyes in the sky! Those who see beyond sightknow when others are watching from the shadows. I felt like I was stepping on her toes (territory) and I knew I didn't know what to do if she cast a spellon me. I was in over my head! So I made a promise to myself to stop!

I stopped doing readings; so when I got back to San Miguel, I immediately went to the Discoteca (the club) and hung out there! LOL my shine was too bright formy own self. I had become too full of "my" "self!" Not in a conceited or arrogant way. It was in a way that I couldn't handle because I wasn't really ready for that part of "me" yet!

When did your greatness first show itself? Did it scare you? Were you ready for it? Did you shy away? Suppress it?

Affirmation... I AM Spirit Giving Birth to Myself... I AM that I AM the Starseed of my 'self' born again into my self's full materialization from the soil of my soul's light... I AM!

Journey To Selfullness

Tassili Ma'at in 1998 coming into her own inner plains initiatory path.

I AM that I AM...I see myself as myself... Starseed

DAY 15

Wow! My greatness was there for others to see, but not me. I was not ready for what I was becoming! And what that was, I didn't know. In fact, all I did know was that I didn't know. So, I decided to do a meditation on the 'no thing.' I was very clear that I knew 'no thing' LOL! So, I did some prantic breaths (yoga breathing). They were deep, long, and full. I began focusing on the 'no thing.' I was breathing in 'no thing' for the 3rd or 4th time, when BAM! I heard this crashing sound ringing and then blackness! The room was spinning, lights began flashing in the space of darkness. I had blacked out and had fallen backward. OMG! That was the 'No Thing' meditation?!?!

I was blown away! If that was the 'no thing' then I was afraid to experience the 'some thing' meditation LOL! The 'no thing' was so powerful, I just sat there on the floor processing what had just happened. I mean I was just standing practicing my deep breathing... I breathed in 'no thing' which was 'something' and literally blacked out. Well, I can't think of a more complete experience of 'nothing' that is really 'something.' I also found out a few minutes later from my housemate, that Mexico City had experienced its largest and most devastating recorded earthquake ever. It happened at the same time I did my 'no thing' meditation.

I'm sure I tapped into the energy field of the earth's shifting tectonic plates. That vibrational vortex and its reverberations knocked me out literally! Wow! So much for being open on both ends. To be so sensitive that I was affected by an earthquake 200 miles away was mind blowing! I was humbled by the power and majesty of the earth and my place in it. Mother Earth has always loved me. She let me climb Her trees, smell Her flowers, swim in Her oceans, dance in Her sands. She has quenched me with Her springs and fed me with

Her yield. I have been enlivened by breathing Her air caressed by Her wind, chilled to the bone by Her snow and warmed by Her love affair with the sun. She is home. She is magic. I AM the two-legged sister to the birds, the fish and the four-legged creatures. I AM the creepy crawlers' cousin. I AM my shadow's twin and my minds' playmate. I AM my ancestors' prayer. Danger and harm always miss me and mine. For that, I'm grateful. I AM my emotion's manager and comforter. I AM my spirit's aspiration. I AM my light'srealization. I AM that and so much more. I AM Starseed, yet I AM 'No Thing!'I AM gratitude appreciating! I AM Selfull! Who and what are you Starseed?

What is your name? ____

What are you called? ____

As for me, I AM that I AM!

Affirmation... I AM Spirit Giving Birth to Myself... I AM that I AM... I see myself as 'my' 'self'... Starseed____(your name) I embrace ALL of me. I unapologetically shine... I AM that I AM!

____

____

____

____

____

____

____

____

____

____

____

____

Ase', Aho', Amen, A'mom...

DAY 16

I acknowledge at least three days of the full moon: the 13th, 14th and 15th day. Sometimes even the 16th when it's a super moon. Calendars are helpful, true but Mother Nature Herself is most reliable. The Gregorian calendar is sketchy at best! Remember what I said in the prologue, it's an agreement, this thing we call time. I mean in Latin, the language from which the calendar was derived, 'Sept'ember is seven and it's the ninth month. 'Oct'tober is the eight and it's the 10th month. 'Dec'ember is 10 and it's the 12th month! Go figure! We won't go into leap year and other irregularities.

Confusion is the name of the day. Some people think solar calendars don't even have a place. But they do because we have a Sun and a Moon, right? It's about balance and accuracy. They are other solar calendars that are waymore accurate. Here are the known top three according to accuracy: The Persian calendar, the revised Julian calendar and the Olmec/Mayan calendar.The Gregorian comes in fourth. Yet we base the whole of western reality on it, this collective agreement of ours. Once again I choose to activate my natural born melanated indigenous woman ways and use Kujichagulia, self- determination. I get more full moon "bang for my buck." That means more time to do wonderful rituals. Back then though, I didn't even know what a ritual was. All I knew was I wanted to have a gathering for my birthday and it just so happened to be a full moon! It seemed to be the perfect time to do it, especially since I wanted to do something different.

So, for this birthday I came to have my first 'Sisters' Circle.' At the time I didn't know that it would one day be called a "Sisters' Circle," I just knew that I wanted to invite all the women that had made a difference in some way in my life. I was at a point that I was really beginning to stand in the fullness of my womaness.

Basking in it! Yet, still loving men and being loved by them. There was no gender question or thought about loving "my sisters myself" in anyway other than platonic. I feel like I have to say that for clarity once again. I've met many sisters and brothers who have confused sisterly/brotherly love with romantic love. There really is a difference. And we can honor and love each other fully without desiring to make love with each other. I'm not going to go into that any further, this is not the book for that. There is no judgment here; to each her/his own. It's just on my heart to put it out there for healing sake.

Anyway, I had a theme party called 'I AM woman giving birth to myself' the guests were asked to bring something of themselves as a gift. It could be a poem or something that they made. It could be food or even a dance. It was so much fun! Everyone enjoyed themselves. Over time, I've had other solar returns where I had women and men as guest in the same spirit of gratitude for their being in my life. It's really revealing when people bring their offerings. We get to learn a lot about ourselves as our friends and influencers are direct reflections of ourselves. How they show up is how we show up, knowingly and unknowingly. Either way it is what it is. The Buddha said it simply by saying "I AM you cleverly disguised as me."

I've grown to know myself by many names, some chosen, most given. All of them true, real, authentic - Me. I AM learning to hold space for all that I AM and all that I AM becoming. All names have been milestones, signposts, aspirations, reminders of myself on my journey to selfullness. I AM that I AM Sheryl Lynn Williams, she who is real, she of Israel, the embodiment of prosperity, The Divine Mother, warrior queen, the Will of I AM, Tamu Ajanaku, Tassili Knight, sweet is the fight for the liberation of African people until death, warrior woman protector, born again as Tassili Night, the heights the highest standard and finest quality one who is keeper of the records through the arts, one who has high spiritual attainment, the ancient one, The queen cloaked in the mystery of the night.

What has your journey been through the meaning of your names? Do you know the meanings? Have you given them meaning, if you don't know? You are remembering what you really already know. What does your name say about you? Given names, chosen names, what agreements have you made with yourself and others through or about them? Remember, all answers are valid!

Affirmation...What are you giving birth to? I AM Spirit Giving Birth to Myself...
I AM that I AM... Asè, Ahò, Amen, Amom, Ameen, In Lak'ech Ala K'in, Ubuntu, Namaste, Medasi ma Nkwa, Nuk pu nu, Ani ze Ani, Selah, Sat Nam... I AM THAT I AM!

DAY 17

The next question for me was: there's got to be more to life than this? So, why am I here? At this point, I had graduated from UCSD with a Bachelor's in fine arts and two minors. One in African history and the other in sociology. I was clearly on my spiritual journey. In fact, it was really the only thing I wanted to do. Just pursuing my spirituality. That was it! African spirituality was still at the root of everything that interest me. Yet, there was no one around in particular to study from. Marva Moore and Dr. Sherifa Saa had both moved from Southern California. So, as always, I let Spirit guide me. I created mojo bags, clothing, mixed media sculptures, paintings, drawings, and performance art. But, while all centered around African art and culture, a more indigenous spirituality began to emerge from within with more power, clarity, and intent. It was actually the part of me that is native to this land... Turtle Island.

I have always felt a strong bond for this continent but I didn't know why. From the African centered perspective, I only related to this land from the fact that we were the first people on the planet. So, of course, we had to have been here, too. But shortly before my maternal grandfather left his body, I found out why. Granddaddy created a family tree that revealed ourNative American roots. My fourth-generation grandmother was full-blooded Shawnee Indigenous. I was told that she and my great, great grandfather metwhile she was on "The Trial of Tears." My great, great grandmother was beingforced to go to the reservation in Oklahoma. Somehow they met. She could 'pass for colored,' as the original natives of this land were very dark with woolly, wavy hair. The light skinned ones passed for white, as no one wanted to go to the reservation. So, when they met, my great, great grandparents ran off, got married, and traveled to Southern Texas. My great, greatgrandmother was a midwife and an herbalist.

Together they had 10 children. Her spirit was strong in me even before I knew of her. As a child, I was always an Indian when it was time to play Cowboys and Indians. For Halloween, I was either an Indian or Gypsy, usually an Indian though. I always loved horses and I loved reading books about Indians and horses. No one else in my family ever talked about our indigenous blood or showed any interest. However, when I look back at pictures of that part of my family, all that was missing was the buckskin, fringes, and feathers.

I learned later that native people who were 'passing' couldn't mention their heritage for fear that they'd be sent to the 'res'... Reservation. So, it was suppressed. Just like the fact that their daughter, my great grandma, Lena, was a seer. I remember as a child, she would have visitors that came over and she would close her eyes and talk to them. She would pray with them, too. When she noticed that I was paying too much attention to what grown folks were doing, she sent me in the other room to watch cartoons. I didn't find out until I was 40 that she was 'reading' them. My uncle told me one night, after he found out I was doing readings for others. SMH! Family secrets! So many things never or rarely spoken. Pieces to the puzzles that make up our lives.

So many parts of myself that I got directly from my ancestors, were just a part of my everyday life as a child. My mom's mom, Gammy, taught me arts and crafts as a child. Little did I know those skills would be what I would use one day to feed my family. I wonder if she somehow knew. Wow! My people really prepared me for this life, my life! I love them so much for that!

How did your people prepare you? Or did they? What gifts, what skills did they give you? Have you ever thought about it? What is your indigenous heritage? Are you, too, from Turtle Island?

Affirmation… I AM Spirit Giving Birth to Myself… I AM that I AM… So, Who Am I?

(Self-assessment)

Because I AM that... I AM Starseed!

DAY 18

I still didn't know why I was here and even after all of that, my life didn't make a lot of sense. I had moved to Atlanta and had married again. This time I thought I was really getting it right, because my second "wasbeen" was 'spiritual' with locs and an African/Hebrew name. He was an artist and to top it off, he was vegan. Never judge a book by its cover. Four and a half years later, after all was said and done, my older sons had gone back to California to live with their father. I had spent time in a monastery and had two younger children. I called that season of my life "Purple Haze" after Jimi Hendrix song he wrote about when he was on an LSD acid trip. LOL!

Yes, I can laugh about it now but trust and know, I escaped with my life. It was a violent relationship mentally, emotionally, spiritually and definitely physically. I ask myself, along with many other people, why did I stay as long as I did? Well the allure of growing spiritually was ever present. The discipline, the knowledge, the intangible jewels attained only from a dedicated spiritual livity (spiritual lifestyle) practice were real. I experienced some of my highest highs spiritually and equally my lowest lows. And yet I knew that if I didn't leave, somebody was going to die and it wasn't going to be me. So, I weighed my options: leave the country, be on lockdown and not be able to raise my children or just leave him and raise my children in freedom. Raising my children was the reality check for me. I didn't love myself enough to leave for me. So, I left for them. I didn't want them to grow up thinking that that was any kind of way to live. No, I didn't want them to think that spiritual devotion meant violence and degradation. So, I chose the latter.

By this time I had grown in spiritual awareness enough to know that my ancestors had never forsaken me. They were still speaking and guiding me and I was finally listening. You see it was from me not listening that I came under the spell of "purple haze" to begin with. Spirit told me in several readings, I had to do five specific things when I first moved to Atlanta. Doing them would have insured a smooth transition. Well, I chose to skip number three. It had the same effect as mixing a cake and leaving out the egg and not using any kind of binding substitute and then being surprised when the cake came out like pudding. So I had to assume at least 50% of the responsibility for the abusive relationship because I didn't listen to spirit and I stayed.

I had created a mess of my life. Many times Spirit spoke thru my children as well and I wasn't listening to them either. Even after I left my second "wasbeen," selective listening got the best of me. Horrible things happened back to back like dominoes. I thought it would never get better. But I kept pushing forward and remembering the Hebrew mantra "this too shall pass." And it did. I begin to share what had happened to me with others. I realized that there were a lot of people, especially women who were being caught in this type of spell in one form or another. So I begin to teach what I called "Applied Spirituality Workshops." I did this so that I could assist others in remembering what it was to listen, to hear beyond sound, to trust their own intuition over someone else's psychic vampirism and spiritual pimping.

So many women and sometimes men were being taken advantage of sexually by healers and teachers who use their knowledge and gifts inappropriately. They preyed on the vulnerability of those coming for healing and seeking spiritual guidance and 'livity.' It was cathartic as their story was my story.

This time when I was called to do 'readings' I didn't run. I began to do readings with confidence and in exchange this time I accepted money. I knew I wanted to serve 'The Most High' by serving others. I knew being a natural hair care professional was healing for the crowns of those whose Ori's (auric field/crown chakra) I cleansed. I assisted so many, especially women transitioning into wearing their natural hair proudly in corporate America. I also knew that the spiritual counseling I did for others, really helped to make some sense of their own lives. I had stopped making jewelry except for loc adornments and sacred amulets. I also begin to do Henna body art.

I was spiritually guided to create Henna Destiny readings. All these different ways to express my creative side was great and helpful to others. I even begin to teach yoga. At this point I had become certified in Kundalini Yoga. It was all very fulfilling too and yet I still felt incomplete. And sometimes even empty. I knew there was more... But what? And why? I begin to have and attended metaphysical retreats. I listened to CDs and watched videos. I went to lectures.I even became a reader for some of the lecturers. And yet, I still didn't know what I came here to the earth, in this lifetime to do.

What about you? Have you ever been at the top of your game, your plate so full that you can't add anymore and yet you still feel like something's missing? Even with all the answers apparently in front of your face, did you still feel like you weren't clear about your purpose in this life?

Affirmation... I AM Spirit Giving Birth to Myself... I AM here on purpose... I came here to (Whatever shows up as your life's purpose. Even if you don't know yet, what do you think it is? What do you like to do and do well?) I AM Starseed. I shine on purpose. I AM that I AM the light. I AM!

I AM Starseed. I shine on purpose. I AM that I AM the light. I AM.

I AM that I AM the acknowledgment...

DAY 19

I was again borderline depressed. Through meditation and Yoga I remembered that as a Spirit having a human experience being on this earth, I AM interdependent. We all are. Yoga means "union," to connect, to bring together." And the word "alone" using word sound power is really "all one." So, I started to think about all that I had to be thankful for. I began to realize how blessed I truly am. I realized that gratitude was what was missing. And that as long as I stayed in gratitude, I will always be connected to life's abundance. I never have to be lonely because I belong to families of beings here on Mother Earth! The Nu Being Tribe! We know who we are, wherever we are! Yes, I'm so thankful for my spiritual family. They have sustained me. Even in the darkest of times, even in the worst of the madness, I could always call on someone or they called me to check in. I was able to go to the sweat lodges and fellowship. I tranced danced, naked around the fire, and bathed my soul in ritual on the full or new moon. I did my own rituals in the presence of my ancestors while silent in my "all one" time.

I was so thankful for my biological family. They loved me no matter what. Even though at times, in fact most of the time, it seemed my birth family and I just didn't mesh. It seemed always a little awkward. I'm sure it was because I was so different from them. Even with my own children it seems like we're cut from a different cloth at times. Especially the older three. So much changed after they went to live with their father; it was almost as if we didn't know each other sometimes. And as for the two younger ones, it seemed as though I couldn't do enough as a mom and a dad. Yeah that's right when their father move to California, I had to become both parents, which was Impossible! I'm not a man first of all. And I really wasn't trying to become one. I mean I can't be and didn't want to be. I was always overcompensating which naturally created more imbalance. All the while, I was still self-employed. LOL! Holding down three businesses and was very active in their school and social lives! My extended family village saved our lives.

Somehow we made it through! They are all grown now. The older three have families of their own. We've been through many ups and downs, but came through it all, healing and loving each other more. In fact, we get closer by the day, hour, minute and second. I'm so proud of my family. Not only do I love them but I actually like and respect them. And I know that's something that not all parents can say. I AM grateful that I can, my progeny; that's the five adult children and my six grandchildren, then my brothers, and nephews and nieces. And, we actually have more in common than I thought LOL! Then there's my extended family, my business and community family. I could not have done all that I have done with my businesses without them. From the customers to the staff, there would be no me without them! Ubuntu! I AM because we are, we are therefore I AM! Wow, if I had to list my greatest accomplishments in this life, it would be my relationships. Especially those with family; Blood first, of course. LOL!

There are a handful of my spiritual and extended family members that must qualify as my sisters and brothers from another mother and father! LOL Ahhhhh... to love and be loved in return! What a turnaround; the missing, was gratitude. I was a thankful person but not grateful enough to be able to appreciate the love that was always there in all ways! The other things or accomplishments have been my commitment to my spiritual path. That's been unwavering and is the foundation for my life. The services I've provided to others, particularly my community, have also been something I can say I've accomplished. Those are my businesses, which have spanned over 40 years. Wow! To be self-employed that long and then to become an actual business owner of an international franchise of eateries using food as medicine is phenomenal to me! And I'm not done yet! And who knew???

Only the Divine Intelligence, my Higher Self, my ancestors and spirit guides etc. I certainly didn't know. And guess what? It's all 'art' to me. I have truly become an artist of life. What I've created as life, is hardly limited to a canvas or inanimate objects. My art is ontological. And I've discovered that I AM here on this earth on purpose to love, to share and be of service to myself and others while feeling good about it! I've finally found self-fulfillment! I AM Selfull!

Think about your life and what you have accomplished? What have you done that was noteworthy? Or what someone else thought that you did that was noteworthy? And it doesn't matter if you're the only one that thought it was.

Affirmation... I AM Spirit Giving Birth to Myself... I AM that I AM the acknowledgment of my accomplishments in the cultivation in the Soil of my Soul...

List them:

____

____

____

____

____

____

____

____

____

____

____

____

____

Journey To Selfullness

I AM Starseed. I AM accomplishment. I AM this that I AM.

I AM that I AM accountable.

DAY 20

So yeah... I had some not so illustrious moments in my life as well. Some art of life that was ugly and that I wish I could've trashed. I hurt some people badly, including myself. I mean I didn't intend to hurt anyone or to be ugly or mess up, but I did. It happened and I spent some precious moments healing, forgiving and asking forgiveness.

The first and worst breakdown in my life was the season of "purple haze." I had never experienced violence in a relationship. Where there should have been understanding patience and tenderness, it was only aggression or violence of some sort. I guess if the person you're with never knew how to be anything but violent when there was conflict, then can they really be blamed for what they didn't know that they didn't know? Most will say yes, yet some will say no. Either way doesn't excuse the ill behavior. And violence isn't just physical. Physical is just easier to see and is most confronting to the touch. Psychological abuse is pretty bad, too. Those are the deliberate games played by the abuser to demean someone else's self-esteem so that they don't trust themselves or others. They will feel disempowered to do anything about their circumstance. They will totally lack the confidence needed to initiate change.

Then there is the emotional piece that has the victim feel like it's all their fault. Like they are the cause of all the problems and that they should be punished. That can look like the silent treatment or its opposite where the abuser is always or frequently speaking in a condescending way to the other, including calling the other person out of their name. It could show up as the withholding of affection or even being shamed for wanting affection. It could show up as the withholding of food, water, and activity such as bathing or being able to go to the bathroom. There are of course other extremes but I'm sure you get the picture. Now, as an adult that has some say-so over your life, if you stay in a relationship like this, then you really do become a part of the problem. That was the case with me. I woulda, coulda, shoulda left after the first hit. But I stayed.

So, I became codependent in the madness, this is not the place for details. That's my next book, "Memoirs of an Urban Mystic." I'm not blaming victims here either. Simply suffice it to say, we are the only ones who can truly save ourselves. How many times do others try to save someone only to have that person turn around and go right back into the situation? The desire for salvation can only come from within, then and only then can someone else assist us in saving ourselves. Once again I speak from experience. I want to be clear here, I AM not even blaming the abuser, however I AM holding them accountable for their harmful behavior. They're almost always abused themselves. You know the saying, "Hurt people hurt people." Well, it's true.

I fell deeper into the abuse abyss when I went to the monastery for several months. I went thinking I would strengthen my spirituality, learn metaphysics and the occult, instead I found myself and my family in a cult. OMG!!! I learned how people get sucked in, trusting others completely, while denying their own internal alarm system saying "GET OUT!"

Kind of like the movie... LOL! I'm joking about it now, but it was no joke when it was going down. And while I went willingly, thinking that it would help my marriage, cultivate spiritual discipline and be a chance to live in spiritual community, it was through that experience that I truly learned the meaning of the phrase "the road to hell is paved with good intentions." Little did I know the so-called spiritual leader was encouraging the abuse in my household, because he was an abuser, too! He was also playing my "wasbeen" and me against each other. It was horrible and it totally devastated me and my family.

This is a classic example of not listening to Spirit. Everything literally said "LEAVE" especially my children but I didn't. I stayed thinking if I just tried harder, I could make it better, I could fix it, etc.

I was stuck in a vicious cycle until we were forced out. It caused a huge rift in my relationship with my older three children. That's when they left to go live with their father in California. I spent many years asking for their forgiveness. It took a long time to forgive myself. I AM forever grateful that they forgave me, however, occasionally something will surface that begs to be healed. And so we do with understanding, patience, and tenderness. In other words, we love our way through it. In fact, there are things that happened with my younger children in the season of "purple haze" that are still being healed as we speak. Life is ontological, ever evolving and we have to learn to get out of our own way! I AM so grateful we have the opportunity to learn how to "grow" through things rather than just "go" through them.

There are a couple more areas of reflection with things that didn't go as planned. The next would be relationships with men who were my lovers, "wasbeens," etc. Don't get me wrong, I love men and I have great relationships with men in general. It's the ones that were closest to my heart that unraveled. In the past those relationships ended up in heartache. In some cases, I just made poor choices while in other cases, life happened. For example, if things had gone the way we planned. I might still be married to my first "wasbeen" and all the children would've been his. But we were young and we eventually grew in separate directions. We had no counseling. And had we stayed together, we would've been forcing an outcome that guaranteed an almost certain probable future of disaster. Yet there is a slippery slope here, because I left and still encountered disaster anyway. It came with different names, height, hairstyles, different complexions, slender or muscular. It didn't matter, I realized after all those years I was involved with the same man! I continue to attract the same type of man. It seemed I was stuck with it, blinded by it, some might even say addicted to it! And the most revealing truth of all, was that I was the common denominator!!! I had to really look deep within and see what I was doing or being that kept me in that loop! So, all the blaming of the men had to stop. I had to be accountable even though they did do what they did; so did I.

I was dragging my past into my future. The final area of breakdown was that of finance. I had no money plan. I just work to pay bills. I would save here and there for things we wanted or needed. But for the most part I had no strategy or plan. In short, "when you fail to plan, you plan to fail." I was just like most people, except that I was self-employed. I didn't understand finance. Nothing was taught about it in school and although my father was in a business that made money, he didn't know how to make money much less sustain it and grow it. I'm sure if my parents had known better they would've done better by me and my brothers to educate us financially, but they didn't so they couldn't. Even with my very successful business, it was so much that I didn't know that I didn't know. Even now I'm still learning through hands-on experience (literally), studying and wise counsel. Finance should be a part of every educational curriculum, just like math, science, technology, engineering, etc. It should be an added "M" to the STEM program, Science Technology Engineering Math Money!

Where have you had breakdowns that impacted your life in a major way? What were some mistakes or things that fell short of your goals? Are you ready to except that you are the common denominator in your life? Remember no judgment... just what happened.

Affirmation... I AM Spirit Giving Birth to Myself... I AM that I AM accountable for my choices in my life. I AM the acknowledgment of what works as well as what does not work in my life. I shine with gratitude for lessons learned. I AM Starseed the common denominator of my destiny... I AM!

I AM that I AM the balance...

DAY 21

When I reflect and I AM completely honest with myself, I wouldn't be who and what I AM if all that stuff good and bad hadn't happened in my life. Fortunately, my heart has always been in the right place. I have always and in all ways did what I thought was the right thing to do at the time. Even if it really wasn't, I thought it was. I just didn't or wasn't always listening to the small quiet voice so patiently and persistently whispering in my head to do the "right thing." The "real" right thing, not the right thing for selfish gain. Or the right thing that was going to keep me from getting in trouble, but would cause suffering and loss to another. Not the telling of the partial truth, when the whole truth is what is being called for. Not the little complaints that planted seeds that grew into weeds in the minds of others. Not the judging without the facts, no discernment. Not the backstabbing, being two faced or being jealous or envious. Not taking things personally, when I knew it wasn't meant that way and even when it was, just letting it go. It wasn't slacking when I knew I could do more or better. Nor was it looking the other way, when someone else is out of order. Nor was it being hypocritical, you know, saying one thing and doing another. Nor was it having the last word, just to prove that I am right.

Now, I realize that all that stuff was really about integrity or the lack there of. Because really and truly "how we do anything is how we do everything." So, because I recognize that I AM Spirit having a human experience, then it's all here for me to experience. In fact, it's a collective agreement forged in the heavens, "Maktub." "It is written" by the hand of Allah. It is a birth contract. Remember? Those contractions our mothers had for us and with us, while birthing us. Yep those! LOL! Each one left its reverberation, its impression of our agreements for this life. What about those who came by C-sections? Many of them still had shared contractions before the surgery. And others? Well, we'll just have to ask them. It seems they are birth contract free, like free moral agents. Perhaps they have no old karma or preconditions of their own, just those made in the moment, as well as those inherited in their DNA. All that set aside and considered, what matters is that "if how we do anything is how we do everything, then if we are always doing our best, giving our best, receiving our best, then the outcome will always be in all ways for the best! Even if we don't understand it at the time. Even if it doesn't look like we think it should. Saying that means, we have to be mindful that our best may vary from time to time.

For example your best will look different if you have the flu than it would look like if you are well. Only you know what your best is. And that's where integrity comes in. It means you're doing "the right thing" even when no one is looking. And if you're not sure what it is, take the initiative to find out. What is the standard expectation? Then meet it and then exceed it. Why? Why not? Even if you fall short, if you've done your best, then feel good. Then inquire to find out what's missing if anything. So, what is keeping you from making your mark? From accomplishing your goal? Never give up for each failure is a foot step toward success. Each breakdown is an opportunity to explore new possibilities. But first you must be accountable. What can you be accountable for? What are some of your perfect imperfections? It's all good.

Affirmation... I AM Spirit Giving Birth to Myself... I AM that I AM the balance... The balance is all the feather seeks... We are perfect in our imperfection... I AM that I AM Starseed... Whole.Complete. Perfect. I AM that I AM my perfect imperfections... I AM!

____

____

____

Journey To Selfullness

Tassili Ma'at is pictured here with some of the Kings that were at her Retreat located at Stone Mountain Park, GA, for the Solstice, 2020

I AM that I AM the feather...

DAY 22

So, let's go deeper; I had to. I was gonna lose my mind if I didn't. It was December, 2007, and I was once again in total despair. You see I danced in and out of 'maintaining' and 'losing it.'

I mean I wasn't on meds, drugs, herb, alcohol or even toxic food. My drug of choice just seem to be a poor choice in men and well, sugar; what can I say? I craved 'sweetness' in my life. I just happen to be looking for love in all the wrong places, mostly outside of myself. I was thankful for my life overall. My children were good, we had a roof over our heads and good food to eat. I had some good friends, The Nu Being Tribe and what I did for work was cool. I mean my life was really pretty much okay. But, just Okaaaay, as once again I was recovering from another dead-end relationship. By this time I had to admit I was a serial monogamist! SMH! LOL! It's funny now, but most definitely wasn't back then. I had a broken heart that left me emotionally and financially bankrupt. And that actually happened a few times. I had lost my passion for life. I wasn't suicidal or anything close to that. It's just that everything was blah. In fact, beige, just the color beige. If you've ever seen me, I AM "the Color Queen," so beige?!? You know I had to be pretty low energy.

To make matters worse after 20 years of being vegan, I began to experience the beginning of arthritis in my fingers. For anyone working with your hands, you know that was a death sentence! I was still grooming and styling locs. I was doing spiritual work and Henna body art as well. With two teenagers still at home, not working wasn't even an option. My world as I knew it was beginning to unravel. All I could do was say "why me?" I was a good person.

I worked hard. I did my best to do right by others. I focused on being spiritually wholesome, exotic, and fun all at the same time! I was a conscious Queen, "Woke" even, yet I felt I had nothing to show for it. Where was my King? And, I never seem to have enough money no matter how hard I worked. What to do???

So, I threw a spiritual temper tantrum right in front of my ancestor altars. I cried and screamed and kicked. I fussed and cussed. I beg them, the Ancestors and the Most High to please let me know beyond a shadow of any doubt what my life's purpose was! So I could be about it, otherwise what was the point of my life? Whenever I looked in the mirror I still saw failure, emptiness and worry. Life just seemed to have no 'real' meaning. Yet I'm not a quitter. I had to go on living, but how? The next day I overheard a friend of mine, Dr. Emikola Richardson, on the radio giving health tips. So I called him to ask him about these arthritis symptoms. Dr. Emicola was an MD, ND, and an herbalist. He was also a Raw Foodist. He told me that the onset of arthritis was caused by starches. I was simply eating too much starch.

I protested, "I'm not eating that much starch." The doctor assured me that that was the case. So to see if he knew what he was talking about, I went a whole week without starches and I found he was right! I had become a starchetarian! I didn't have enough fresh leafy greens, vegetables and fruit in my diet in general. Along with not drinking enough water turned everything into paste around my joints. Uuuggghhh! After that week of no starches all the pain and stiffness went away. And like most folks, I just knew that I was cured. Which of course meant that I could go back to eating what I was eating before. Right? Lol! So what did I do? I made spaghetti! And after three days of eating it, the pain and stiffness was back. I knew the seasons of change were upon me. Raw foodism was the next level for me spiritually and now it seemed physically for the health benefits. I was faced with a complete lifestyle change. Or not, I mean I could've just continued doing what was familiar like most folks. You know, doing the same thing over and over and expecting different results. I was tired of that! I have been doing that and it was almost always the most certain probable outcome - Arthritis.

I had been introduced to raw foodism back in the mid-80s when I had gone to Mexico with the Institute of African Mysticism. It was there that I met one of the founding fathers of the Raw Food movement, Dr. Aris Latham. Aris is "Sun Fired Foods." He lives in Panama now and I invite you to Google him. Dr. Latham is a living legend. I owe my foundation for the fulfillment of my life's purpose to him, my raw food guru. So I committed to a "live-it," (not a die-it) for one year. I committed to only 98% raw, though instead of 100%.

Why, because I live in a city that gets cold in the winter and fall. And I want something hot sometimes. The environment doesn't really support being vegan, much less raw. So not wanting to be stressed out about food, I created a workable standard for myself. I also didn't want to feel guilty if I did decide to have something hot, nor did I want anyone else trying to guilt trip me about it. It was exciting and very inspiring to create raw dishes. The colors, textures and aromas were so healing. It was edible art! My passion had returned!

In the meantime, I had recommitted to my yoga discipline as well. My yoga teacher told me that if I wanted to clear my love relationship karma, then I should abstain from intimacy for 18 months, so I did. That's when I began to have a deeper relationship with myself. I didn't realize how much I didn't know about me. I began to create myself a new! I was able to look myself in the face again without sadness. I could see the sparkle return to my eyes. I wasn't a failure. I was on my journey to 'within.' When one begins to be sustained by life giving things like foods, activities and a measurable way to see improvement, one can be truly alive. Look in the mirror into your eyes. Do you like what you see? Do you love yourself Starseed? Honestly, are you living honestly?

Affirmation... I AM Spirit Giving Birth to Myself... I AM that I AM the feather and the heart of the soul of Starseed only myself first only itself first. I AM that I AM my truth... I AM!

Journey To Selfullness

I AM that I AM the heart...

DAY 23

I began to do mirror work and had some deep heart-to-heart conversations with myself. I had to be honest with myself about everything in my life and my part in it. I forgave myself and others. That was probably the hardest thing to do, forgiving myself. Why, because I felt like I should'a, could'a, would'a done better if - If what? What was my intention? Who was I dealing with? When was it going down and where? I didn't know what I didn't know. The real questions were what did I learn? Did I grow? Am I healing? Can I do anything about what others said, did, or thought? No. I couldn't. So all I could do was work on me. I could also be a resource for others when they needed it. I realize the richness of my life through being of service to others. Coming full circle once again brought me to that clarity. Sometimes when we're so rebellious, so hardheaded things have to be revisited over and over again before it really truly becomes a part of our conscious awareness.

I love this analogy because it's exactly what Selfullness is. On an airplane when the stewardess says "If the oxygen mask drops down, put yours on first then, help the person next to you." So, first I made sure myself and my children did our yoga every morning. We also read from The Book of Changes and The Unchanging Truth. It's also known as the I Ching. In my opinion as a result of my studies, it's the Taoist version of MA'AT and an unofficial eastern version of IFA. This stems from my acknowledgment that all spirituality was and still is one. Organized religions have caused spirituality to be morphed into a myriad of different expressions, most conflicting, some harmonious, I'm always seeking the harmony. My children and I also meditated for 15 minutes to top it all off before getting ready for school. That set the tone for the day and became our daily due diligence.

What was almost a tragedy, the arthritis, became my saving grace. Changing from a 'diet' to a 'live-it' inspired others. People could taste the love in my food and immediately loved it too! Before long I was vending, catering, and selling food from my home. I used texting to advertise my daily menu. I sublet several places in the Historic West End of Atlanta, before finally having my own brick-and-mortar at 1059 Ralph David Abernathy Blvd., Southwest.

It's called Tassili's Raw Reality Café. We opened January 1st, 2011, on Imani the last day of Kwanzaa. Faith, the meaning of Imani, is exactly what my journey has been based on. The knowing and belief in the fulfillment of something that is not yet seen or happening. I was finally clear! My current purpose and ultimate one, is that of being of service as a healer. In the restaurant, we use "food as medicine, deliciously." I watch our guest come in and after eating our food immediately and always over a long period of time they are transformed! They are on the road to healing and well-being! The Most High and my Ancestors let me know beyond a shadow of a doubt this is exactly what I'm supposed to be doing. It was truly a calling!

Affirmation... I AM Spirit Giving Birth to Myself...The heart is heavy, unless one takes themselves lightly... I AM releasing shame and embarrassment by learning from the sh*t of life. I AM the knowledge that is the fertilizer reconditioning the soil of my soul... Life is too short not to shine, Starseed. Intentions of a pure heart are those nurtured in the richness of the Soil of the Soul's knowing of mistakes and misdeeds done. I AM that I AM learning to fertilize and grow out of the sh*t! I AM!

Journey To Selfullness

I AM that I AM the integrity...

DAY 24

Even my lack of money didn't stop me. In September 2008, I took $250, my dad's matching $250 and opened 'Tassili's Raw Reality' inside of 'Healthfull Essence Caribbean' vegan restaurant. That was only possible because of Ujima and Ujamaa, the third and fourth practices of Kwanzaa. The third practice of Kwanzaa, Ujima, collective work and responsibility was the only way I could've done it. My children, nieces and nephew helped. My friends joined in and worked for food as well. That was where the fourth practice, Ujamaa, cooperative economics came in. They believed in my food, me and my vision of a global Empire where food is used as medicine deliciously. Fortunately, Princess, the owner of Healthfull Essence, was open to Ujamaa and gave me the opportunity to get started. Even before that, Adio Akil asked me to help her establish a raw food component in the newly opened vegan restaurant, called Paas at the beginning of 2008. Paas was started by a woman named Manana. She was one of Dr. Sebi's students.

Adio was a long time student of Dr. Sebi as well. Some of his teachings rubbed off on me, too. In my solitude, I acknowledge that even the situations that caused Adio and I to fall out and then later me and Princess to fall out were absolutely necessary. While they were very painful, Tassili's Raw Reality Café never would have become what it is without all of that sh*t that I went through. Out of it all, I emerged shining! My brand stands on its own integrity. I don't compromise quality, flavor, or a standard of love. Which by the way is the main ingredient in all of Tassili's Raw Reality Foods. In fact, it is my very essence that is in the food. It is Tassili! It is the highest standard and finest quality! I AM the Sh*t! LOL that's real transformation! What sh*t have you transformed in your own life? What was the sh*t that happened that caused yourtransformation so that you became the Sh*t!?!

Affirmation...I AM Spirit Giving Birth to Myself... I AM that I AM the integrity of my shine. The integrity of my shine is found in the accountability that my Soul is nurtured in... Alone in my own sh*t, I AM acknowledging the "ALL ONENESS" of it all. I AM Starseed. I AM that I AM the sh*t!

I AM that I AM acknowledging...

DAY 25

I have become somewhat of an urban legend now as a result of using food as medicine, deliciously. And from being a grassroots entrepreneur turned Mogul. Many are inspired and have found us to be 'the' bridge to assist them in getting from where they are to a state of optimal health using raw vegan food. I AM because we are, we are therefore I AM. My service to African people is primary and after that anyone else can benefit. I make no apologies for that, as there is no need to defend that which is just the right thing to do. And anyway, how could I go somewhere else and tell or help someone else to clean their house and mine isn't clean?

I'm going to start at home first and that's my commitment to my community! Furthermore, freedom fighting is in my blood. I came to observe that it's better to live for freedom, justice, and well-being, than it is to die for it. And in fact, when I look at the health of our freedom fighters, it's frightening, sad and very discouraging. When I observe how many have died, not from assassination by guns or lynching or beating, but by a slow and debilitating death, that actually was self-induced, I AM appalled. How? Biological and chemical warfare!

The diets of our people guarantee an almost certain probable outcome of painful death. Not from dying naturally, because it's their time. But because they have strokes, high blood pressure, heart disease, diabetes, lupus, cancer, etc. All of these are preventable. These are modern diseases that have natural remedies starting with the food. All that our freedom fighters fought for, worked so hard for, is being given right back to the institutions that they were fighting against. They become co-dependents of the death industry. Eating processed foods, fast food, mostly fried foods, cooked to death foods, which cause them to deteriorate early in life. Then they begin to spend their hard earned money going to the doctor's offices. And then come the pharmaceuticals. Then the hospitals, the insurance companies, with their high premiums, and that's even if they can qualify and can afford it.

Ultimately ending up in the funeral home leaving an almost insurmountable amount of debt for their families. That's right! If they hadn't paid that debt off, then their children are strapped with it before they can even begin their own cycle of debt to the disease industry. If that's not a generational curse, I don't know what it is. Many say it's too expensive to eat healthy; well in fact, it's cheaper. Either way, you're going to pay something; so why not invest on the front end, rather than pay on the back end of your life. That way you are investing in prevention and your future generations, leaving them a legacy of well-being. But it does require some effort on their/your part. Start reading labels. Google the info and question it. Get several definitions if necessary.

I would recommend reading, but I know most people don't do much of that anymore. BTW, thanks for taking the time to read this! Listen to audio books. Either and any way, feed your mind. Also ask yourself, how do you feel when you eat certain foods? How do you feel when you don't? Don't judge yourself, just start paying attention to what you do and why. For example, what are you thinking about when you are craving that red velvet cake? Did you just have a fight with your boss or did you just get a promotion? The goal is to "know thy self." After all, you are the only one you're going to be with your whole life. Even your life partners, parents, and friends will never know you like you know you. Become your own best friend. Get to know you and love you! Give up what no longer serves you, embrace that which does!

What are you willing to give up as your commitment to your life?

What are you willing to begin and grow in, as a commitment to your legacy and your future generations? Are you willing to live for freedom, justice and wellbeing?

Affirmation… I AM Spirit Giving Birth to Myself... I AM acknowledging. I alone as the "ALL ONE" Know what is workable and what is not… I AM that I AM my observations... I AM!

I AM that I AM seeing

DAY 26

In September, 2016, I completed the Landmark forum. It was amazing and I truly learned to get out of my own way. How? By first seeing that I was in my own way to begin with. Lol! Landmark is a remarkable personal and professional development curriculum, developed by Werner Erhard. My take on it is that he seems to have studied all the spiritual paths available to him. Then he took them and stripped them of all their "isms and schisms." He left the one thing they all have in common, spirit/truth/integrity. Then he repackaged it and branded it as EST and then later Landmark.

Because it has some of all spiritual paths, people of every background can relate, even atheist, if they want to. Nothing is forced and if one participates, one can really have a quickening in breakthroughs in their lives. If they go and just sit there, they'll still get something, just probably not as impactful. But who knows, maybe they will. Either way you can't unlearn, only change or transform.

So the seeds of transformation get planted and people have the opportunity to begin to think outside of the box. They can discover the root causes of what holds them back in life. And they also learn how to use 'the distinctions' 'tools of communication' to help them learn how to get out of their own way. I had some very powerful breakthroughs, such that I've continued to take other courses through the Landmark curriculum. I found the communication courses have been truly the most transformative for my business and my family relations. That is of course, after the forum, which is the initial introductory course.

It has impacted me so much that I created a scholarship for my staff to take the courses. And it's mandatory for my upper level management as a professional development opportunity. One of the biggest breakthroughs came through right after I took the forum. I finished on Sunday and flew to Egypt the very next day.

It was my first time on African soil. I cried. I went with Dr. Muata Ashby and his wife Karin Ashby. They have written over 70 books about ancient Kemet. Exploring its spirituality and its culture from an African centered spiritual perspective. This was a spiritual sojourn for me and the others. We spent six out of our 10 days there at the temple of Seti I. Seti I was known as the Philosopher Pharaoh. His temple was totally dedicated to the enlightenment process. The hieroglyphs or Metu Neter (the utterances of the Gods/Divine) showed scenes from birth to Godhood. Step by step, hieroglyph by hieroglyph, and pictograph by pictograph "the way" was shown. I could hardly believe what spirit showed me next.

I could see and hear that the landmark forum was a modern way or path toward enlightenment! What! That's crazy! Yet I saw it with my own three eyes, heard it with my own ears as SEBA MAA and SEBA JAA (the Ashbys) read and deciphered the Metu Neter on the temple walls! Spirit spoke to me in the inner sanctum of my being. I saw beyond sight "a way." The Metu Neter/hieroglyphics were there as the "what" and Landmark was there as a "how." It's certainly not the only way to enlightenment. I would never say that. But I must acknowledge "what's so" for me. The landmark technology is taken from our ancient sacred sciences. Anyone who has studied both can see it. I invite you to do the same. Study, participate, learn and grow. Even all the yoga, meditation and spiritual studies haven't given me such a powerful quickening like the Landmark weekend. All of that spiritual work however did prepare me to optimize the experience though. It also prepared me for the sojourn to Kemet and for the Temple teachings. I'm so thankful for all those dots being connected. I AM becoming whole. What discoveries have you made on your life's journey? What were some amazing almost unbelievable connections that came together, opened up new awareness for you? What have you seen beyond sight? What have you heard beyond sound in the inner sanctums of your being?

Affirmation... I AM Spirit Giving Birth to Myself... I see... I AM Starseed as the light that I AM... I turn to my inner eye introspection... I enter the spectrum of my inner sanctum... I AM that I AM my first eye. I AM!

DAY 27

I own my life now. I mean it's always been mine, but I didn't know how to claim it. I didn't know what or how to value myself, my experiences and what is now my knowing. To be able to except and love myself unconditionally is something wonderful. To know that the world is just a little bit better because I've been here is empowering. To realize that I've only just begun to really walk on the solid ground of confidence it's comforting to my soul.

I have learned to be really kind to me. I am so full of love for myself now unapologetically so that I have plenty of love to share with others. For that I am so thankful. I've even learned the difference between being thankful, grateful, and appreciative. I'd like to share this introspection with you now. Thankfulness stems from feeling good about something intentionally done on our behalf from another or vice a versa it's reciprocity, a give-and-take. Something is expected in return for the balance, not a good bad right or wrong, just a balance.

Gratitude (A great attitude) has all to do with being greatly filled with the acknowledgment of unconditional giving (love) that we are the recipient of from others, known and unknown. For example, being grateful for air, we benefit but don't have to do much to get it, only exhale. The trees then take the carbon dioxide and transform it into carbon monoxide. We just breathe while they do the majority of the work. Gratitude is a deeper level of being thankful, there is still reciprocity but not consciously or necessarily expected. And appreciation is when you pay your gratitude forward because you can. This is because you really value what you're grateful for. You give without any expectation, even though you know what you put out comes back. So like investing your money, you appreciate your gratitude by being kind, etc. And like money when you invested it returns in-kind as your ROI. You know the world, someone, or something is better because of your appreciation. I had avery deep lesson given to me by spirit such that when I got the lesson of gratitude and appreciation, my relationship to money and prosperity transformed.

I will share it because it's a classic example of appreciation. It started from within. So, this one day, I was having a pity party all by myself. I was complaining that I had to do EVERYTHING all by myself! I was so alone and woe is me! Now here we go. I'm looking out of my window complaining about doing everything by myself, as I was watching my children get out of my friend's car. She and I had a carpool going to get our children to and from school. That small voice, that 'something' said, "You are so ungrateful. You've just energetically spit in the face of everyone that's ever helped you!" This time the voice wasn't quiet either, it was a full on conversation. It went on as I sat there with my mouth gaping open. It spoke again, "What do you make, Tassili?"

Did you make your clothes, did you grow your food? Did you pick your children up, did you make the car they arrived in? Did you drill for the gas that got the car here? Did you build your house, did you chop the wood used to build it? Did you make the tree, did you make the air? What about fire and water, did you make them? And dirt, what about that? Did you make any of that by yourself, Tassili? In fact, what did you do by yourself, Tassili? That's right name one thing. You weren't even born by yourself! Shut up! Get grateful! Wow! I was speechless! I had always thought of myself as a thankful person. In fact, I knew I was, but apparently not enough. I seemed so ungrateful at the moment that I questioned myself about what gratitude even was. It was simply the acknowledgement of all the things I AM thankful for that I take for granted. It's recognizing just how blessed I really am, unconditionally with no strings attached. And you are, too!

So, you will rarely ever hear me say that I've done something alone because I rarely ever have. There's always, in all ways, been 'something' there helping me, providing for me in ways upon ways that I don't even know that I AM provided for and yet somehow I know that I AM. I AM now showing appreciation by sharing this with you! Thanks in advance for receiving this! So, go deeper, Starseed. Are you a thankful person? What are you grateful for and how do you show your appreciation? I go into the Endarkening...

Affirmation... I AM Spirit Giving Birth to Myself... I go into the Endarkening. I see beyond sight... I reflect my inner light into myself... I AM the sacred sanctum of the Soil of my Soul... I AM reflecting the inner realms of my Starseed Self. I AM that I AM!

DAY 28

As I prepare for this next phase of my life, I appreciate my journey by sharing it with you. I AM now asking myself these days, what's next? The expansion... the global expansion of course! I AM in meditation receiving Divine guidance. I AM in conversation with my advisers. I AM in concert with nature, at a jungle mountain retreat, checking in with myself, as I complete 64 revolutions around the sun, in this lifetime anyway. And I've only just begun to explore the places prepared for me in the reverie of my mind's eye. I have conceptualized, visualized, actualized, and materialized all that is now being realized. I AM grateful to create the places and spaces for others to follow, while building platforms for others to lead. The peace that comes from almost completing this task is growing. Preparing has been more than a notion, yet it is being done. Tassili's Raw Reality has been just that.

A raw, fresh, and at times crazy reality; it's been a bittersweet journey. When I look back, who knew that I would make a $1 out of $.15 - LOL! That a $250 investment and my vision would one day become a multi-million dollar ROI. If someone had told me what I'd have to endure, I don't know if I would would've done it, which is why "Something" just kept pushing me forward. Showing me only what to work with: the best quality, (specifically kale) fresh, locally grown, organic, non-GMO, raw, vegan and transitional foods available.

Then, what the end result would look like, food as medicine, deliciously satisfying a hunger the world didn't even know it had! And finally the purpose is to be a global bridge assisting people in getting from where they are to a state of optimal health by nourishing the body, mind, soul and spirit.

Those were reasons enough to keep me going, to keep me persistent, tenacious, persevering, determined, undaunted, driven, compelled, passionate, and focused. I stayed the course. I'm so glad I listened. I'm so grateful for my ancestors who shoulders I still stand on. I'm about to cry now, as my solar return completes in the country of Belize. I said "no more winters in the cold." Look at me now!

How did I make it through? Well, definitely not by myself! LOL, My mom's spirit was who I called on when my breast was bleeding and in pain from stress. I called on her again when I could barely walk from the long hours of standing every day all day, resulting in neuropathy in my feet. I thought of the future generations, my progeny and those of my staff. I thought of all of those who helped along the way, kept me going when I had full-blown shingles, was losing weight, exhausted and had to open every day on time regardless.

My earthly angels, the "Kendrick Family Credit Union." Wow! They are a prime example of community in action, Ujima, Ujamaa and what 'real' Christians are supposed to be! They saved my life helping ends meet through barter and service! OMG! The first three years being late on rent almost every month, but I never received an eviction notice! Thank you, Sam Baycote, my unofficial silent partner. And thank you Lisa for supporting Sam in supporting me. Thanks Sam, also for saying that I reminded you of your grandmother, Lottie Watkins. Her example as the first black woman millionaire in real estate in Atlanta was most definitely an inspiration. I called on her spirit quite a bit, too!

Mr. R. Thomas, of R. Thomas Deluxe Grill in Buckhead, was one of my first mentors. He kept his doors open for me giving advice and sometimes even financial support. Then there was Ifni and Mr. Mac, her white Lincoln Continental. Mr. Mac drove us everywhere until he couldn't drive anymore.

So Many doors opened because of you, my SiSTAR, including Sevananda! (Even though we have gone our separate ways, one day we will come again to heal our wounds.) The list of opportunities go on and on as a result.

I'm remembering the time I was making African carob cake after being open for one month at 1059. I was transported back to my five-year-old self, making mud pies and realizing that now I AM getting paid for making edible mud pies! Not only that but naming "what's hot and spicy, sweet succulent and juicy like every woman wants to be and every man wants to experience! And it keeps you coming back for more... The Punany wrap, that is! LOL! This along with the open cashbox and condiments on ice. SMH! LOL! Using the Tassili Money/barter to pay for "The Hotspot" from 11:00 PM to 4:00 AM on Saturday nights and live music for Sunday brunch.

"We make the rules–dant, dant, dant-we make the rules!" Chi Ma'at, Jessica Starchild, and I sang loudly and proudly as we marched around the restaurant, not realizing how true that statement really was! Tassili's Raw Reality was an industry disruptor. And then me, as a guest Chef on Royal Caribbean cruise liners, four times! And guest chefing in Bimini at a healing retreat. Our early events,"The Return of the Gods," "The Goddess Retreats," "The Days out of Time," and "Kundalini Rising Yoga Retreats." "The Healers' Alchemy," the Inipi withKwame Sunhorse, and fire walking with Baba Reed, too. "The I AM Ascension Temple" and yoga classes weekly. "The Natural Mystic Fair," and, of course, "The Wonderful Wizards of Raw." Russell Simmons' "10 Laws of Success" andthe books "88" "Think and Grow Rich, a Black Choice and "Sacred Commerce" kept me focused and anchored even when most frustrated.

I can't forget the music, I had ringtone reminders by Guapalè: "Closer," Beyoncé: "I Was Here," Jill Scott: "Golden," and Gil Scott: "95 South" original and the remix. These kept my eyes on the prize! What was the prize? "A healthier planet, one bite of kale at a time!" Who was I? "Ms. Independent" by Ne-Yo. One of my mottos in the first few years was "money before honey."

It kept me abstinent for 22 months, with fewer relationship distractions afterwards. Rapper TI promised if I took care of TRR one day, "I could have whatever I like!" Even before the brick and mortar, D Train's "Sky Is The Limit." "You know that you can have what you want, be who you want, just keep on pushing on." Can't forget Raury's "God's Whisper," which helped me spiritually fortify once I got the brick and mortar.

Coming full circle with the music and accomplishment, I achieved a monumental milestone stone in creating my reality when after being open for five years I remembered the song "Psychedelic Shack" by the Temptations and how as a child I would ask my mom if we could go there. She repeatedly told me it didn't exist, so we couldn't go. Well mom, I created it! Yep I realized I had a "Psychedelic Shack" at 1059 Ralph David Abernathy Boulevard.

How powerful is that? It's really located on the street name for one of our freedom fighters, in the middle of Chocolate City USA! It's almost heaven. We say Atlanta would be heaven on earth if it had an ocean. But then it wouldn't really be Atlanta, or would it be Atlantis transformed? I would be remiss if I didn't mention some of the brightest Starseeds of my journey. My aunt Margaret left me an inheritance, which I invested into the restaurant so we didn't have to go get another Square loan. Shout out to Square! They were game changers in making the difference from an institutional contribution. Thanks to Daddy and Caroline for all of your support while in your bodies and out.

Thanks to my two youngest children, Khaajit and Arata, and my nieces Aziza and Chi Chi. They all swore that they were born into indentured servitude. Lol! There was some truth in that. They had no choice especially my children.They had to help. They had to earn their keep. I wanted to be sure they had good work ethics. Then there's Adio, Manana, Princess, Octavius, Tracy, Abba Shaka, Kaya and Baratunde, Mahti, Baba Hassan, MBali, Shabazz, Jennifer, Yoshi, Ish, Robyn, Mark, Jimi, Tawa, Sheriese Nicole, and Astarius. And, of course, all of the new admin crew: Fred, Koo, Miriam, Thalia, and Zoie Dawn. I just knew I'd be turning it all over to you, especially the five people that I trusted with my business, money, heart, soul, and life. I just knew this season of my journey was about to be complete! However, I AM forever grateful for the good, the bad, and the ugly!

You know the saying, "Do you want to make the Divine Intelligence (God/Goddess) laugh? Tell it YOUR plans!!! It's been said many times that there is a side to the Divine Intelligence that is the trickster, the practical joker, and sometimes impractical. Yep, just when I thought I was done, obviously ready to release it all, the Divine and the Ancestors called me back. They said "You ain't going anywhere - not yet!" It was late February 2020 and Covid hit the world. In the beginning of March, I received a call late one Saturday night from my broker Elijah. He said, "Ms. Ma'at, your company is being embezzled in the amount of what seems to be 400K within one year!"

I was speechless and numb. "Wait! What? How? Who? When? Where? And Why?" These questions surged through my brain. I immediately called my God brother who is a Babalao; a priest in the Yoruba tradition of Ifa. He did not live in Atlanta nor did he know any of the people on my staff. All he knew was that I had a restaurant. In fact, he and I reconnected only three days before.

I asked him to consult the oracle for me, and what Ifa revealed was the identity of five people. That was ALL of my upper level management. OMG! Clearly my whole world was devastated! I have been spending the past year and a half stabilizing my business, recouping my sanity, and putting protections in place so that it will never happen again. Trust and know that justice will be served.

And what was my accountability in all of this? I wasn't inspecting what I expected. I didn't know what I didn't know and when I hired the people to do their jobs I trusted them blindly to do it. There is nothing wrong with trusting others, just never trust blindly. And truth be told, I was also burnt out from the journey of building the business, family turmoil, and transitions. So, when I saw and suspected shady behavior, I did not check it. I did not want to believe that the people that I trusted with my life and livelihood would have behaved in such a way. But they did. It was even more hurtful because they could have just asked for the money. I had given several of them large sums of money from my own personal savings, not to mention loans and bonuses from the business. Justice will be served! Karma is real. I had to go deep into the Endarkening to pass this test. This was the ultimate test of proving my spiritual disciplines and tools to do the work.

I have to give a special shout out to Teresa and 'Waking Up Well.' That's where she performs her magic. She heals the healers by holding space for us to heal ourselves. I must also mention Eli and *StudioSteffanie* for 'their boots on the ground' helping to hold the business down while going through this transitioning. I would be remiss if I didn't mention once again my beloved family, who all came to the rescue to save the business and their legacy! To all of my spiritual, business, and community families, I can't thank you enough for your continued love and support. I AM boldly stepping into the future embracing it all!

To all of my haters, you're my motivators! I thank you too! Because of you, I AM stronger and shall win in the end because it is my destiny. No weapons formed against me shall prosper! I AM that I AM truly grateful for my life! They tried to bury me, but they didn't know I AM a yellow self-existing Starseed. It is my galactic signature! I AM humbled by the sobriety of self-acknowledgment and fulfillment! I AM Selfull!

What say you, Starseed? What in your life's journey is almost complete? What torch are you passing on? Who helped you along the way? What about your journey made you smile?

Affirmation… I AM Spirit Giving Birth to Myself… I meditate, contemplating my own reflection of darkness and light… I AM the mystery of my soul's soil 'mystory'… I AM my journey. I AM that I AM gratitude and appreciation… I AM!

Tassili Ma'at meditating during her Journey to Selfullness in Belize
at the Pyramid of Altun Ha on January 21st 2012.

I AM that I AM full moon womb Black wholeness...

DAY 0

Ummm, I say that I AM now complete, well almost. There's really still more to do; in fact and in truth, more than can ever be done. LOL! So remember, don't worry, just do what you can. It all works out for the better anyway. Part of my Landmark training has taught me how to spot and cultivate a leader. This part of the preparation is in process. Trust plays a big part in being able to turn your 'baby' over to someone else's care. In truth, Tassili's Raw Reality isn't a 'baby' anymore. Yet and still whoever is going to take charge must be qualified. Recognizing another's strengths and weaknesses, while appreciating them, allows for the appreciation of my own. Steel sharpens steel is one of my mottos. Being able to release, give up, make room for, move on and grow, is all in alignment for me, although sometimes it is a little scary. I must be fearless, clear, and come empty so that I can be poured into continually by the Divine and my ancestors. I AM making room for new platforms.

Founder, Creative Director, and Expansion Visionary. I AM preparing for the next level... "TRRUEE G!" That stands for "Tassili's Raw Reality Urban Economic Enterprises Global." Wow! And the journey continues! I AM whole, complete and perfectly happy with myself and my life. Freedom and ease are ever present even in the midst of adversity. I choose to choose them. In fact, they are my constant companions. I AM so full! I AM Selfull! And no more serial monogamy, LOL! I'm ready for the divine love relationship with the love of my life! These thoughts and stories that I've shared have hopefully inspired you in some way. I'm so excited to be able to share my "Journey to Selfullness" with you! Some of it I know, most of it is still to be discovered. When one door closes another one opens!

Journey To Selfullness

As a disruptor or better yet a unicorn with wings, I keep one of Jay Z' sayings close to my heart, "I bust through glass ceilings and kick down closed doors," just in case I ever get stuck again. This time, however, it will be different. I will remember what the stewardess says when she explains the safety rules "If the oxygen mask falls down, put yours on first, then help the person next to you." Just another way of saying, "Be Selfull!" I trust you have been journaling along the way and will freely reflect back on our journey together while completing this lunar cycle. Who have you identified as leaders in your life? What have you been willing to give up to be empty so that you can receive? When doors are closing, what new doors are opening up? Are you fearlessly ready to walk through them? Are you Selfull yet?

Affirmation... I AM Spirit Giving Birth to Myself... I AM that I AM full moon womb Black wholeness... I AM that I AM Complete... Giving birth to my Starseed Self Anu... I AM fulfilling myself... I AM that I AM Selfull!!... I AM!

I invite you to continue journaling your Journey To Selfullness - 365.

Journey To Selfullness

Journey To Selfullness

Journey To Selfullness

Journey To Selfullness

Journey To Selfullness

Journey To Selfullness

Journey To Selfullness

Journey To Selfullness

Journey To Selfullness

Journey To Selfullness

Journey To Selfullness

EPILOGUE

I give thanks for the opportunity to be your Urban Mystic Guide on the Journey to Selfullness! The journey of remembering what you really already know. I look forward to continuing our journey through my books, workshops, and retreats where we can go deeper into the endarkening. This is where the shadow work dwells so that our inner light or enlightenment can shine through even brighter. Together we are a Super Nova! "Let the circle remain unbroken!"

In truth, In light, In love, Tassili Mata Atma Ma'at

Tassili Ma'at and Erykah Badu sitting on the front porch of Tassili's Raw Reality Café located at 1059 Ralph David Abernathy Blvd., Atlanta, GA 30310.

Made in the USA
Columbia, SC
14 July 2024

38222677R00135